LIVING
KINDLY

Bold Conversations About the Power of Kindness

Essays Collected by Leigh M. Clark

Aurora Corialis Publishing

Pittsburgh, PA

Disclaimer

Dedication

To my son Carter, seeing the world through your eyes reminds me of all the kindness and curiosity the world affords us.

To those who've supported and coached my journey from day one, I appreciate your love, patience, and belief in what is possible. This wouldn't be possible without your kindness.

Advance Praise

Kindness is magic, and no one knows that better than Leigh Clark. Her exciting new book is an inspiring collection of stories that will give you all the feels and make you want to do better, be better.

Meaghan Murphy
Editor in Chief at *Woman's Day Magazine* and Author of *Your Fully Charged Life*

~~~

Despite what you hear on the news, human beings have an enormous capacity for kindness. Because of what you hear on the news, we need to exercise this capacity more than ever. This book offers lovely examples of people leading with kindness, and a reminder that change begins with all of us.

Jamil Zaki
Professor of Psychology at Stanford, Director of the Stanford Social Neuroscience Laboratory, and Author of the Bestselling Book The War for Kindness: Building Empathy in a Fractured World

~~~

Kindness is the key.

It does not surprise me that my friend Jo Davis is involved in a book about kindness. She is an extraordinary woman, who has lived a life of deep and immersive experience, full of feeling and growth.

My own journey as singer, songwriter, peacemaker, advocate and the last member of The Supremes has been a ride through pain, growth, and realization that kindness is the true spirit and purpose of our lives.

Living Kindly is a testament to the journeys of changing paths, which arrive at kindness as a way of life. This is a time of deep worldwide growth and change, and never has a testimony of kindness been more needed or worthy of our attention.

Bravo to the writers of this wonderful book. Kindness raises its beautiful head and moves forward powerfully throughout our world, because of this book.

Susaye Greene
Former Member of The Supremes

~~~

A glimmer of hope. . .

In a world seemingly riddled with incessant pressure and persistent negativity, *Living Kindly* emerges to prove just how gentle and bright that world really is—and the unlimited potential we possess to spread that kindness, even in the darkest times.

The collection of experiences inspires readers to commit even the smallest act of kindness and uniquely portrays the humanity that resides in all of us. What better way to prove how good-natured the world really is than with honest stories of ordinary humans who bring purpose to their lives (and others) by simply being kind.

Nicolette Emmino
Director of Storytelling and Host at Insomnicat Media

~~~

Living Kindly is for you guys!

I've known Angelica, one of the coauthors, for nearly a decade, and she has been a very strong anchor for me during my dark periods and has pulled me out of it numerous times.

I was particularly touched by the story she shared in *Living Kindly*. For someone as cheerful and bright who can go through something like this, all of us are susceptible to the same thing. But it's comforting to know there is someone out there that can help those who have felt the same pain of heartbreak.

During the pandemic I went through one of the darkest periods of my life, and I can definitely relate to having those bad thoughts and blaming myself because it's the easier route to take. But Angelica is right, you have to love yourself and show up for yourself first before you can for others.

Hrush Achemyan
@Styledbyhrush

~~~

Living Kindly is a reminder that where kindness flows humanity grows. This book highlights how an act of kindness can change the world. It is so needed in a time when we just don't see much kindness toward each other and people have grown not to expect it.

Kathi Muhammad
Founder and CEO of Serving Women Across Generations

~~~

In reading *Living Kindly*, I learned that kindness is a verb, and an unconscious and conscious mindset not to be taken lightly but requires action to be taken. This collection of stories brilliantly takes you through the gift and journey of kindness. This is what the world needs more of.

Orlando Haynes
Author, Speaker, Career Growth Advocate

~~~

I lived as a grade A perfectionist for years until I burned out. Having been constantly driven to perform, to achieve, and to seek validation from the outside world I overlooked my own needs and desires. The blessing behind my burnout is that it led me to the world of self-compassion and kindness on the deepest level. I discovered that being kind to myself is not only an act of self-preservation but one of generosity. Sharing from the overflow of my life force energy means I can graciously serve others.

The stories in this book highlight the inner transformation we enjoy as we practice kindness, including being kind to ourselves. This is a message so needed in our world now!

Andrea Pennington, MD
Author of *The Real Self Love Handbook*, Founder of The #RealSelfLove Movement

~~~

This book beautifully maps out how kindness can be infused in our lives every day, for today's and tomorrow's leaders.

In times when individuals are struggling with social justice issues, the pandemic, economics, mental health, and uncertainty about their future due to challenging circumstances, this book is timely. In the chapter "A Kind Journey," Krystle Mabery lays out a path for transformational change and servant leadership. I found her words in particular to be not just a very inspiring read, but also creative thoughts on how to take ACTION in serving our community on an individual level.

Living Kindly is a must read for everyone involved in human rights issues . . . and aren't we all?

Dr. Zakiya O. Mabery
Author/International Speaker/ DEI Consultant
CEO of B. Global Diversity and Inclusion Strategic Planning

~~~

Kindness is undoubtedly an undervalued, seemingly intangible commodity. The contributors have shown without a doubt that kindness is actually a valuable, quantifiable thing capable of changing lives and enhancing the planet. For instance, in the chapter "Kind Hearted: How I Healed a Broken Heart," written by my friend, colleague, and spiritual counselor Angelica Perman, a decision to render unrelenting self-kindness following a romantic heartbreak showed the powerful transactional value of kindness.

Kindness to ourselves is generally the last thing most of us consider a priority. However, as recounted, self-kindness is actually the first step in healing both ones' self and our community. While many individuals, families, businesses and groups have been ruptured by the pandemic, the very essence of an energetic exchange based on kindness elevates oneself immediately and enhances the overall quality of the environment, the community, and the greater world at large. As Angelica did unto herself, so she does unto the greater tribe, multiplying kindness' effectiveness in immeasurable volumes. She also elevated her own goodness, talent and productivity.

If we each follow the same self-kindness protocol, our planet inevitably would be healed whole and continue to be a sparkling point in the everlasting universe. It is brave to be kind to one's self. It is also, in fact, necessary for humanity's evolution, the greater planet at large and actually our greater galaxy itself.

This book should be read because it shapes how we move in the world as doors, homes, and relationships are re-opened in post-pandemic days. While a light reading, its chapters positively shape personal, professional, and community relationships.

Diana Marcketta
Documentary/Docu-series Producer and Creator | Former Journalist

Table of Contents

Illuminating the World with Kindness

Leigh M. Clark

There's a light within each of us that sometimes dims and flickers. With hope, we can let that small, dim spark grow. Each positive experience we have makes our lights a little brighter. There are some fortunate enough to practice an attitude of being grateful for those moments enough to gather them up and shine a bit brighter. Those who continue to focus on the good allow the light to radiate from inside them out into the world.

My own beginning felt dim, but the future has never been brighter. I can already see the light shining in you, and that means we are continuing to illuminate the world through kindness

From One Act of Kindness to a Movement

Like so many in 2020, I had big plans. I had my first book coming out that coincided with my first ever TEDx in May. Everything was lined up perfectly, and then I was reminded of the unpredictability that is life. It became incredibly silly and out of touch to care about that when the world was turned upside-down by the pandemic that overwhelmed the globe, and my book *Succeed With An Impact Mindset (SWIM)* was swept away. My once important moment in time became a problem that was insignificant in comparison to the way the world was suffering.

When we all came up to the surface sometime late in the fall (if only briefly), I was met squarely with the understanding that the world needed *more* than a book about our individual evolution. The world needed light. The world needed kindness. Kindness is the core of my soul and the beat of my heart. I became ready to answer the need for kindness, but I didn't realize the voyage it would take.

Today that voyage has landed in your hands.

I thought that the world could use multiple perspectives on what kindness was and how we could find it within ourselves and muster up enough of it to perhaps share it with another human. So I decided to share my book with other humans. We needed to bond together, stripped of any ego, and give our servant hearts to the world. Just one question . . .

Where would I find these people?

I did what any tech business woman would do. I headed to Linkedin. But I thought, *What do I search for? Perhaps "Global Kindness Crusader with time to write"?* Instead, I decided to keep it simple. I searched "kindness" and then clicked on people brought up by that search, and that would forever change my life—and hopefully yours as well.

The search returned very interesting humans, who an algorithm had decided exuded kindness, but it was far beyond what I had envisioned. I found people running kindness businesses, corporate kindness consultants, kindness executives, professors in kindness, and so much more. I sent a very basic message to them stating my vision to create a collection of voices on kindness to bring their light and perspective to an anthology I wanted to create.

I was worried that no one would be interested. Then it dawned on me that *these people are kind*. They *live* to help others, like me, both in my busy career in technology and through my role as chief kindness officer at the nonprofit I launched years earlier.

Not only were they willing to take the call. They sprang into action. They were engaged and excited and wanted to make a difference. Combining this team with a few kind influencers I had met over the years created the cast of *Living Kindly*, the book you are reading right now.

Your purchase of this book, by the way, will go on to help us design acts of kindness across the world in the countries and cities the authors lived in. We were all excited to get to work, and we began to learn more about one another. The stories that emerged were insightful, interesting, and moving. The bonds that began to form across the team would be the foundation of much more than this book . . . they would become a way of life: living kindly.

Some of the authors knew my story and others had never known me before I wound up in their messages. My story is one that may start like yours . . . with one small act of kindness.

If we rewind to twelve years ago, you'd find me unemployed, living with my parents. Amidst the recession, I lost my job as a director of marketing. I was devastated as my corporate climb was what I felt defined much of my worth. I was living in New York, wearing important shoes, and thought I was headed for the American

Dream. Life then would laugh heartily at me, for probably the first time in my adult life, although clearly not the last.

I wound up too broke to make it in New York—like boiling my water for a bath, couldn't afford my parking tickets kind of broke. I made the call and moved back to my parents' home in South Carolina, realizing I was fortunate to have a place to go but still sad that my dreams and purpose felt dashed. I would spend the months ahead trying to figure out how to get back on my feet.

Being somewhat new to adulting, I threw myself a giant pity party and stayed a bit too long. I wallowed in my shattered ego. I squandered my time. The days seemed endless. My mother would say, "You have so much time. Why don't you volunteer?" I just didn't have anything in my heart to give; honestly I wasn't just broke—I was broken.

Eventually, I found my way back to a good corporate gig in a new state, starting the slow climb back to balance. Still, my soul was pretty drained. My financial and emotional reserves were gone. I was unhappy and felt I lacked purpose. I'd find, in the years ahead, that purpose and happiness were directly correlated.

The following winter, I couldn't seem to find joy or get into the holiday spirit. I was overweight, underwhelmed, and pretty bored. But somehow, I made what ended up as a life-changing decision: I decided to do a 30-day mind, body, and soul cleanse.

Each day from Thanksgiving to Christmas, I would do a juice fast, a 90-minute hot yoga class, and a random act of kindness. It's clear now, even if it wasn't then, that even on my darkest days, I am a bit "ambitious."

It is a huge understatement to say that the first few days were hard. The yoga classes felt like burning torture, and I missed chewing immensely. The highlight of each day was the act of kindness.

Since I had no idea how to get started with my "random acts" and didn't have much money, I knew I'd have to be creative with my acts of kindness. I dialed the local chapter of a large U.S. nonprofit that coordinates resources to organizations and people in need. I asked if they had any daily volunteer shifts or places to donate clothing and household goods. They gave me great advice on where I could pitch in.

I still didn't have a ton of extra money, but I had saved a couple bucks to do something special.

One day, I walked into a local store and asked if I could pay off someone's layaway. The cashier's face lit up as she scrolled through to choose a layaway with a balance that was just the amount I had to give. She then picked up the phone, calling the recipient to tell them that someone had paid off their holiday gifts. You could hear the woman's excitement through the phone, as the associate smiled and nodded. I never felt so great, doing a small act of kindness. I was instantly hooked . . . and I wanted everyone else to experience what I'd felt. Why had I never heard how much euphoria giving could give someone? They should charge for this stuff.

Although I made it through the 30 days, the juicing didn't last beyond that, and neither did the hot yoga. The kindness did. Giving transformed my life. I tapped into a joy that I hadn't really known before. My inner spirit transformed. Every aspect of my life improved. Giving became part of my soul. Now, it's a fundamental part of who I am.

I began to share the kind acts on social media, in an effort to inspire others to do the same. I hoped it would bring them joy too and, in turn, joy to the lives of those they affected with kindness.

I remember early on, long before the kindness pages emerged online, that posting about nice things I did was perceived by some as self-serving. I overheard snickers of gossip from judgement-passing onlookers like, "Who does nice acts and then posts about them? What does she want? A cookie? A trophy?"

It hurt. It also forced me to look deep within my intentions to ensure I was doing this for the right reasons. Was it worth the scrutiny? Upon reflection, I became strong in my resolve. I knew when I did the acts of kindness I would do them quietly, not wanting the recipients to see me giving. The intention of my online shares was to pass along the good feeling I'd discovered in giving, and let others know about this fantastic mood booster I'd discovered.

I wished I'd taken my mother up on her volunteering suggestion years prior because it felt great to give back. Before that, it sounded like giving back was for the wealthy and the saints. I was tired and uninspired back then, so that was the last thing I felt motivated to do.

Maybe you can relate to that feeling, when you're depleted and don't think you can give any amount of yourself to someone or something else. What I would uncover, though, would forever change my trajectory.

Kindness became such a big part of my life. Initially, I needed to find a way to fund the acts of kindness I was carrying out. I didn't have a lot of resources, so I launched a small art line called "Kindleigh Art," whose proceeds went to the initiative. My friend Terri and I would sit at the farmers market every week in the blazing Florida Sun hoping to make enough to at least cover our booth fee and hopefully a bit more to do something kind with.

That art line would become a nonprofit called "Kindleigh," centered on random acts of kindness and putting positivity into the world. We then launched our Kindness Community, which grew to over 26,000 members in 46 countries in less than 5 years on both Facebook and LinkedIn. We grew our team to include kindness attendants, admins, ambassadors and volunteers who were all overjoyed to get involved and shared the things we were doing with their local communities nationwide.

Before you knew it, our little organization was featured on *Rachael Ray*, *The Today Show*, and many other outlets, including the pieces I was writing on *Huffington Post* that featured some of the kind acts we were up to. Things like passing out flowers to strangers, collecting toys and school supplies for foster kids, distributing backpacks full of crucial items for the homeless, gathering food and supplies for victims of natural disasters, buying Valentine's gifts for women and children in domestic violence shelters, and much more . . .

It's hard for me to even believe that we've now shared kindness with nearly 15 million people globally through our acts, campaigns, groups, and news stories. We were best known for the Holiday Acts of Kindness where we carried out an act of kindness for individuals and other charities every single day of the holiday season, year after year.

Within that, we created #payawaylayaway where we fundraise to pay off strangers' layaways across the country—an act that's very special to me. It was one of my first, and I remember thinking, *I'm not like "Oprah rich," but maybe if I got some friends together, we could eventually do something bigger.* Each year, it grows and so does my heart, knowing that a little light from within me could shine so bright onto others.

Although I've carried out countless acts of kindness across the past decade, I want to share a couple of particularly important ones with you that I've never shared publicly before.

Santa's Sleigh

A couple of years ago, I was planning our annual holiday acts of kindness when I was tipped off by somebody helping a couple in need. These two lovely individuals were living in a trailer, and the wife was a double amputee. They were really struggling. I was informed that they didn't have enough money for Thanksgiving and asked if we could help in some way. I thought this was a great act of kindness to kick off the season.

I went to the grocery store and got them everything you could want at your table for a true feast with all the trimmings. When I walked through the door of their home, I met Jackie and Ken. After talking for a few minutes, I thought that these are such amazing people who are just having hard luck. Jackie talked to me about how much she used to help people before she became disabled and how many people she thought would always be there for her because she was always there for them.

Then Jackie said, "You know, when things got hard and when I lost my legs, it was sad that no one I talked to could take care of us. We don't have any friends and family who visit. Nobody calls. Nobody helps us out. It's disappointing that all I gave to others was never returned."

I sat on the floor with their dog and bonded with them for over three hours that day.

When I left, I knew Christmas was right around the corner, so I promptly decided I wanted to make it a really special one for Jackie and Ken. I wanted to surprise them with a magical holiday!

We worked hard to get them everything we could possibly think of, new blankets and home decor, makeup and perfume for Jackie and a shaving kit for Ken, dog food, new dishes, and a few big dog bones for their dog . . . and much more!

Christmas day—with my Santa hat on—I loaded my sleigh, and off I drove with my other kindness elves to deliver Christmas. The delight on Jackie's face when she opened the door was like the pure bliss of a child seeing a beautiful gift.

She was just so delighted and excited! She said she hadn't seen a Christmas like that in her entire lifetime.

We went through the gifts and spent some time together, and Jackie told me how much it meant to her to have somebody show up for her.

Then, I said, "You told me that nobody was there for you after you had been there for so many. But I'm here for you. Perhaps it's not the ones who you gave to over the years who are here for you, but *know* that you deserve everything you've given and more."

We stayed in contact on Facebook for some time, but later that year, I was saddened to learn that was her last Christmas. It warmed my heart that she left this earth knowing that kindness is never done in vain, although you may not expect it, it is always returned in ways unplanned.

This feeling reminded me why we do what we do. This heartwarming feeling is what happens when you reach people, when you see their human need and take some kind of positive action. These are the feelings of joy when you make sure that people feel seen, valued, and heard.

Ballet in Rainy Paris

Our organization usually doesn't take requests. We do what we call "random acts of kindness," meaning that we do different initiatives, projects, and campaigns. There's an endless amount of need out there, and although we would love to fill requests, it would overwhelm our organization.

As I mentioned earlier, we had developed a community on Facebook for our organization, and we were really growing and had thousands of members at this point. At that time, we allowed personal fundraisers in the group.

I noticed that a particular group of people was posting a lot of Go Fund Me links. That seemed odd.

I'd come to find out later that they were trading in diapers for their own personal gain and that "several people" was actually just one person. I swiftly removed them from the community. But I stayed bitter about it in the days that followed.

I wondered how people could take advantage of kindness.

How can people ask for more than they deserve and take it out of somebody's hand who really needs it?

I hated that I felt this way about something I worked so hard to build, but I felt jaded and disconnected. I felt sad witnessing the darkness in this world. Maybe I'm an optimist, maybe I'm naïve, but it hurts my heart.

A few days later, I received a message in my inbox from somebody I had met at a seminar years before. She was in a bad position and humbly asked me for help. I knew her personally and I knew that she lived in my area. We had changed the rules for the Kindness Community so no one could post personal fundraisers because they were too hard for us to verify their authenticity. This woman, however, reached out at the perfect time. I needed to have my hope restored and remember that people out there need and deserve the light.

This would be the only request I would ever take, and I would take this one personally.

She was in a shelter with her infant daughter as well as her adolescent daughter.

She said "I'm finally about to get out of the shelter. I have an apartment lined up through the housing authority. But I have nothing, I have no furniture, I have no dishes, I have no pots, and I have no pans. Can you help me and my daughters get a couple of necessary items for us to move in?"

Again I decided this time I was going all out. I did not post about this mission in the Kindness Community or as part of the charity, but on a personal crusade, I decided to take it to my personal page and ask friends to pitch in.

I asked everyone in the area if they had any old furniture, TVs, pots and pans, or anything of the like that I could get together for this woman. The offers poured in for couches, chairs, barstools, and pictures. I asked the woman what kind of paintings or artwork she liked because I know everyone has a different style for their home.

She then told me she never owned a painting. That saddened me, and I realized it wasn't a necessity to own artwork versus paying a bill. It was a luxury to be able to fill a blank wall.

So I asked, ``What do you like? What can you envision?"

She said "I love drama, and Paris, and ballet, and I love, you know, creative things and beauty."

I knew exactly what I would do: I would paint something for her. I decided to paint an acrylic of a ballerina at night in the rain in Paris next to the Eiffel tower with the water splashing off the streets and the gold lights of street lanterns lining the street she was on. I put so much love into that painting! I was so excited to give that to her, more so than even the furniture that I was using to furnish the apartment.

I had called her to see if she was ready to move in and started scheduling deliveries. Unfortunately the government is a little slow sometimes, and her move got delayed. Her heart was broken because she would have to say "no" to all of these pickups and deliveries because she had nowhere to put them.

I decided to continue to help, and I wondered after being recently taken advantage of if I was doing too much. What would happen if the storage unit was needed for more than a month?

I have faith that everything happens for a reason and to trust the timing of your life. So I got her a storage unit. We went there and filled it with furniture day after day, her daughters riding along on the moving carts laughing, giggling and having a good time.

One of my local friends asked her children to donate their toys to these little girls. They also chose to give up their allowance and give that to the family as well. It was so sweet.

We showed up at the storage unit, and she was so thrilled to see all of the things that people put together to get her started on her new journey. I handed her the painting. When she unwrapped it, her head lowered, and her eyes got glossy. I could tell in that moment that she really understood that somebody wanted to take care of her heart to make sure she felt loved.

Eventually the housing opened up, and we moved her in. She was so happy to be in her new place safe with her daughters. But the story didn't end there.

I wanted to get to know her better, hang out, and have lunch. I could just tell she had a good soul. I respected her and admired the courage she had to reach out for help to take care of her family.

We are still friends to this day. She is one of my closest friends, and I am so proud to see all she's done since that moment at the storage unit. I can't say much more than that to keep her story confidential.

Through that act of kindness and the things that have transpired since, I felt my bitterness about those who schemed the generosity of people dissipate. The goodness in her extinguished the darkness I had seen in others. With that, each time I experience negative forces, I think of her and realize it's just my reminder to continue to shine more light and to help others do the same.

I'm so grateful that our organization continues to grow and affect even more people. We don't ever give a hand out. We always give a hand up. I know that I found my purpose with kindness, and this little light of mine . . . I'm gonna let it shine.

Now let's meet some of the people that light touched who are blazing their own bright light across the country and across the world. These are the authors who trusted my vision and our organization's mission enough to loan you pieces of their soul and perspectives on kindness.

Shining the Light: Living a Legacy of Kindness

Neil Schambra Stevens

They say there are four major stress triggers in life: losing a job, the bereavement of a close family member, marriage or divorce, and moving to a new house. I experienced all four of these within 12 months, and that was in the middle of the global pandemic as well.

"So, what has this got to do with kindness?" you may ask.

I learned lessons from these significant moments, both as individual experiences and as an overall perspective.

I learned the importance of gratitude, of seeing the simplicity of things, appreciating the everyday, observing the things that are in our control and letting go of those that are not.

I gained resilience, understood that "indeed, this will pass," and knew that there is a cycle of light and dark, day and night, and I needed to just breathe in this rhythm, trust the process, and keep my resolve.

In a similar vein, events like these ensure that we maintain momentum, one foot in front of the other, one step at a time, that we are able to shift our perspectives slightly to reveal things in a new light, sometimes pausing to accelerate.

And finally, to focus on kindness.

To clarify, I am not suggesting that there was an absence of kindness until this point in my life. In fact, it was the opposite; I realized, however, that much kindness was ingrained in my everyday perspective and how I had been brought up with kindness as a core family value. By leaning into this deep pool of kindness and its close sidekick love, I was able to navigate these challenges, and even to thrive and grow.

Sometimes, everything needs to completely fall apart and unravel for you to realize where you are truly meant to be in life. Despite how one might respond to these events from the outside, the lessons and my learnings from this time provided me with strength, energy, and a direction to move forward and to seek and explore something new. So, let's take a step back to break down some of these key moments, the impact they had on my thinking, and my journey to where I am today.

When my last job ended, I took time out to reflect on what's next, to dig in and think about what I was truly passionate about and investigate the clichéd expression "What's my 'why'?" It was also during this time that my relationship became increasingly challenging and went into a hasty decline. They say these things happen slowly, then really fast, and I can vouch for that.

As the end of my marriage involves my ex-wife and two children, it is not my story to tell alone. The only observation I would share is that the absence of kindness in my relationship propelled me to go the other way and seek and appreciate the goodness and impact that being kind can have on an individual. Kindness is a nurturing and uplifting force, simple in essence but impactful to both give and receive.

In the pursuit of my why, and to gain further perspective on what I wanted to do next, I set up regular "coffee conversations" several times a week. This was pre-COVID and in-person and seems a distant memory under our current circumstances. These conversations were with a mixed group of like-minded souls, creative industry contacts, and new connections I had reached out to as I was curious to hear about their own story or purpose. Increasingly, I realized that my interest was drawn to people and teams and, in particular, how to support young leaders in business. But at this point it was not clear how or what this support looked like.

I had been really fortunate to have enjoyed some amazing professional opportunities working as a CMO/VP with Fortune 500 brands and corporations, including Converse, Vans, Lenovo, Levi's, and Polaroid. Although I'm originally from the U.K., my career path has enabled me to collect life and work experiences along the way across Europe, Asia, and the United States.

How could I use this journey and these experiences that I had collected over 20 years to help the next generation of business leaders? I continued to explore and investigate, asking enquiring questions to my coffee companions as the seeds of an idea started to form, even if it was not 100% clear what it actually was yet.

Then in September 2019, my father suddenly passed away.

I say "suddenly"—he was 90 years old and had suffered from Alzheimer's disease for about 10 years—and yet it still felt like a shattering jolt out of the blue with a phone call from my sisters that he had passed away peacefully during the night.

Part of the preparation for his Thanksgiving service entailed contacting the various former companies he had worked for and the professional associations he had been a member of. My father had a lengthy career working as a chartered surveyor in the City of London, including being president of the Royal Institute of Chartered Surveyors and acting as an external industry advisor to the U.K. government at the time on various business rating and taxation issues of the day. Serious stuff . . .

And yet, the overriding sentiment from the multitude of messages of condolences the family received was how my father always came to work with joy and how he always put people first. Here is one such example from a former coworker.

"Jim and I shared an office with David at 15 Arthur Street for a couple of years, and to this day I've never encountered such a wonderful, kind, and encouraging fellow worker. He always had a smile, participated in daily 'banter,' and had a great sense of humor. Every morning his arrival was a joy."

Another one of the many stories we received that resonated with me was the occasion when my father had to present a particularly complicated case to the district valuation officer. During the case summary, the officer fell asleep! Upon waking up he glanced over at my father and concluded that everything was in order and that they should move ahead with the proposal my father had made. Knowing that the officer was not aware of all the details and would probably get into trouble for a) falling asleep and b) accepting the offer without fully comprehending the proposal, my father suggested that they split the proposal 50/50 to make things even, which the officer agreed to.

In the car on the way back to the office, the junior associate who was present during the case was furious and demanded to know why my father had not accepted the officer's decision to accept the proposal. My father's response was "You can take an advantage in business, but never take an unfair advantage."

These stories and many similar others struck a chord with me. It was the trigger I needed to fully appreciate the importance of putting people first and the significant role that kindness plays in business as well as everyday life. In fact, it reminded me that there is no distinction; we should treat everyone with kindness, whether it is in our day-to-day or in the workplace and at whatever station people are at in their life.

It was in that moment that I realized that I had found my why.

Recognizing this revelation during a period of intense personal sadness had a duality to it—Reflecting on all the goodness and kindness that my father had bestowed on the world yet also realizing that he was now gone was hard to reconcile.

There was the comfort of knowing how much joy and kindness he had brought to people's lives both personally and professionally and also the pain that he would not be contributing anymore, that his "kindness quota" for the world was now complete. But what to do with all that kindness he had so willingly bestowed onto the world, be it family, friends, colleagues, and even strangers in the street?

I used this double edge of thinking of how I could honor his memory and contribution, combining it with finding ways to build on his good work by bringing joy and kindness into the workplace. It was during this period of reflection—and dare I say grief—that I started to think about my father and his own upbringing.

My grandfather was born in 1899, making him a proud Victorian. The values they grew up with in terms of faith and family provided a solid foundation before they experienced the horrors of World War I and the subsequent economic hardship of the 1920s. It was in this backdrop that my father grew up, and despite the circumstances of what would have been a difficult transitional period in history, home-life was full of love and laughter, joy and kindness.

My grandfather was a true "gentle man," always immaculate in collar and tie, impeccable manners of the day, raising his hat when he passed a woman in the street. He had a calmness and resolve, almost unflappable but with a keen observational eye on life. He was a man of few words but those that he did share had a charm and eloquence to the extent that our family still uses many of his expressions today. Indeed, it is this oral tradition of kindness that I wish to maintain when we are so overly consumed with soundbite culture, absorbed by motivational quotes in an "Instagram-minute" before moving on to our next fix.

By contrast, my grandmother, born in 1900, combined a warm and generous heart with a steely determination and disposition and was more vocal in speaking up for those who maybe needed a hand or a voice. She had an innate sense of right and wrong and ensuring justice prevailed, especially when she felt people had been treated unfairly or unkindly. In fact, she often referenced a tapestry that hung in her home that stated, "I shall pass through this world but once. Any good things therefore I can do or any kindness that I can show let me do it now for I shall not pass this way again."

I first read this tapestry as a boy in my grandmother's house, and these words have always resonated with me. The words and sentiment are so relevant today, especially with the fast pace that business currently moves at combined with the impact of social media, constantly fueling our desire for more content as we mindlessly scroll from post to post.

What if we took this as an opportunity to become more present and become more kind as we "shall pass through this world but once"?

What if we recognized the importance of being in the moment, particularly at work, and made a commitment to ourselves to be kind, and to be kind now, knowing that "I shall not pass this way again" and practice kindness every day and everyday kindness?

My father's empathic approach and inherent sense of treating people fairly and with kindness is one of my inspirations for starting Mercury Jam, and my grandmother's tapestry inspired the "Contract Of Kindness" that is at the heart of my coaching and strategic programs. I have taken immense pride in continuing my family's values of kindness and supporting others and treasure having used its energy in helping to discover my "why" to push things forward.

How could I connect the legacy of my father's approach to kindness to the contemporary business world, our current ways of working, and a new generation of employees with potentially different values and priorities?

Firstly, I needed to have a sense check for the acceptance or doubt that kindness has a place in business and to ensure an impactful approach. Knowing that kindness is a mindset and an active choice, it is therefore key to use the right tactics to achieve this meaningful goal of kindness as a force for good in business. Tone, language, and reciprocity are essential in this regard.

For some, kindness resonates naturally from an emotional perspective. Others, however, need a little more persuasion, and consequently, many of us use data and research to support the value of kindness at work. Thankfully, the ranks of like-minded souls, aka "Kindness Avengers," are swelling gradually, and there is now strength in numbers, as the Living Kindly group is testament to.

I have always believed that people work for people. They are the #1 asset in your company. When people feel secure and appreciated, they perform better. Many perceive that fast-paced frenetic processes and work cultures lead to more risk taking. In fact, it is the opposite. Good leaders need to create a calm, secure, and safe environment to give people the courage to take risks. They need to know you have their back. When you have a kind, positive working environment, people come to work with joy. Joy fuels effectiveness and productivity. It builds loyalty and retention. It all starts with kindness.

In a calm, secure working environment, people are willing to go further, to explore more with a positive impact on personal development and company growth. There are fewer days of absenteeism and, consequently, less of a strain on other team members and resources. Kindness is ideal to unlock growth in both your people and your brand. Who would not want more joy-filled, productive people in their organization?

Sadly, there is still the perception that somehow kindness is a weakness in business.

Hold that thought . . .

It is widely recognized that kindness is an enabler to calm, supportive working environments. Such environments inspire trust and loyalty and reduce burnout. By comparison, toxic cultures cost companies billions of dollars each year.

The average cost to replace an employee through burnout is $120,000 due to loss of productivity, onboarding, training, and team impact. Yes, I said, "average cost." So, if the words, deeds, or actions of one toxic employee—be it a peer, co-worker, or leader—triggers 5 or 10 people to leave your company, that one toxic employee has cost your company over $1 million. Is that toxic employee so valuable to your business that they lose you that much money every year? I think not.

Another critical factor to highlight is the scale of the issue.

A pre-COVID Gallup study of 7,500 full-time employees found that 23% of employees reported feeling burned out at work very often or always, and an additional 44% reported feeling burned out sometimes. Meaning 67% or two-thirds of full-time workers experience burnout on the job at some point.

We should also consider the fiscal impact and loss of revenue attributed to absenteeism from burnout. The World Health Organization calculates that work-related depression costs the global economy $1 trillion in lost productivity annually. That is the equivalent of 91 million sick days worldwide every year. *Every year.* And that was before COVID-19. Definitely nothing to be joyful about . . .

These issues should be red flags to all CEOs, especially as, according to a recent Bloomberg survey, 65% of employees do not believe their senior leadership takes proactive steps to create a healthy, kind workplace culture, meaning only one in three are recognized as being proactive. With these sobering statistics in mind, it's hard to see how kindness could ever be considered a weakness. On the contrary, it's rocket fuel for business, improving the mental mindset, morale, and connectedness of the organization and therefore having a positive impact on the output and overall productivity.

So, what's next for kindness? Like a lot of social issues today we are up against the clock.

COVID is a once in a generation moment. For a time, in early 2020, it felt like the entire world was knocked out of kilter. Never before had basic health, safety, and sanitation been put front and center as our daily lives and routines were upended. It was a time of uncertainty and fear as we were forced to retract into our homes and reduce physical contact with our family and friends.

Articles about well-being and mental health flooded newsreels and posts. Despite the anxiety-inducing headlines, many people saw this time as an opportunity. Not an opportunity to take advantage of people's pain, suffering, and grief, but more to reach out and say, "Hey, this is hard right now, but it will get better." As we look ahead, we have a chance to start over and rethink the way we engage with one another. There has never been a better time to share experiences and collective knowledge. Now is the moment to establish some codes of practice for how we treat one another and work together.

We can make kindness the "new normal."

One approach to inspire these new practices would be to gather large groups of CEOs and senior learning and development executives together to share data points and research and inspire a trickledown effect.

They could be triggered into action by highlighting the benefits of kindness to productivity as companies hit hard by the pandemic seek short-term gains to get back to growth. There is an urgency that many do not seem to recognize. When employees lack the joy and motivation to perform well, then the efficiency of the company and the overall energy to succeed is impacted. The time for action is now.

Despite some positive soundbites you may have heard, less than 8% of Fortune 500 brands have allocated meaningful budgets to implement the broad church of well-being practices in the workplace. Senior leaders, if you do not start addressing these root issues, you will not have an environment that empowers your people to feel good and perform at their best, and no amount of ping pong tables, bean bags, or free snacks in the cafeteria will fix that. Start to allocate and invest appropriately in kindness now. Given that three out of five employees who have been with their company for eight years or less say they'd change employers for a more positive, kinder culture, there's no time to lose if you want to retain your best mid-level talent.

Another approach is to reach out directly and appeal to a generation of workers such as Generations Z and Alpha, which are already tuned in to more empathetic views on world and working practices, to inspire them to build a foundational mindset rooted in kindness and gratitude, and by using enablers such as momentum and resilience.

I am striving to create an impact on well-being and productivity in the workplace by leveraging kindness as the catalyst. I do this by shining the light on emerging talent and next-gen rising leaders. My personal definition of kindness is to enable people to be seen, to be heard, and to be valued, and in business, that starts with the up-and-coming talent.

My observation and experience from corporate life is that a lot of organizations focus on the top of the tree with executive leadership, offering training, support, and paths for career development and fast track schemes.

Granted, not everyone has the ambition or skillset to be a senior leader. However, I see the opportunity in working with the middle management, those on the rise, those still finding their voice and learning how to navigate their authenticity in the business world. Here is where we can create impact, to inspire a mindset of kindness as an active choice, to recognize the value of daily gratitude and instill the benefits of maintaining momentum and resilience. With these four values in place, we can nurture a positive vibration globally.

When you have a positive, kinder working culture, people show up to work with more joy. Joy fuels productivity. When your people perform better, your business performs better. Loyalty and retention increase; burnout and absenteeism are reduced. You can measure the growth in your people, not just in the profit of your brand.

Isn't this the kind of organization we want to build?

Don't we want teams of well-rounded individuals, juggling the balance of their personal and professional lives, feeling that their input and contribution is valued?

Employees who feel motivated and self-empowered, enabling them to move forward with speed and kindness?

A lot of companies encourage employees to stay in their lane and "color within the lines" which can be hard when you are in this transitional phase of self-discovery as a leader. From direct feedback from colleagues, clients, and mentees, this pressure to conform and stay within the lines is a particular challenge from a gender perspective, with the additional social pressure on women to navigate many outdated expectations or stereotypes from traditional patriarchal organizations.

My response is to encourage them to, yes, "color within the lines," as I am not advocating anarchy or rebellion here! Instead, I am advocating for them to use their own crayons to express themselves in an authentic, open way that is true to themselves.

For Gen Z, growing up being radically inclusive and empathetic and openly caring about the world and social issues, this notion of being true to themselves not only increasingly resonates but is expected as the norm. Leaders need to acknowledge this potential generational divide in approach within teams and organizations and work harder to not alienate generational groups. Instead, they must use the power of kindness to bridge the thinking to establish more future-facing brands and companies. It's how you establish a culture and legacy of kindness throughout the organization.

My goal is to shift away from the traditional metrics of success and achievement in the workplace. Naturally, revenue and growth are key to the health and buoyancy of a company. After all, employees need compensation and benefits.

However, my ambition is to establish true "Kindness KPIs" (key performance indicators) to gauge well-being so we can positively impact productivity. This could be targets for reducing absenteeism and burnout rates, targets for increasing referral rates ("This is a great place to work!"), or focusing on retention rates and celebrating employee milestones. These would be elevated as an organizational priority, not just buried somewhere in an HR handbook.

Senior leaders would be actively required to share KPIs of how kindness had a positive impact on a particular team, function, or department's performance as part of a quarterly business review. This would be presented alongside the traditional revenue metrics to demonstrate the health and well-being of the company on an equal par with its profitability.

And what about future-proofing the organization for success with the next generation of leadership? When companies are creating their talent development programs and succession planning, the kindness quota potential of an individual should be established as one of the key critical factors. Current leadership planning revolves around functional performance solely aligned to growth and revenue. Surely there's space to add in some metrics around kindness, gratitude, and resilience as hallmarks of a future empathetic style of leadership. Remember, it's all about the people.

People are the single most important asset in any brand, company, or agency. Before your product or your service, it's your people. Without them, nothing happens—you do not have a company, just a name or an idea. Companies need to refocus their commitment to their people. To show kindness, empathy and understanding. It is how you inspire people and build loyalty.

My children are 11 and 13 years old, a girl and boy.

They will be entering the workforce within the next decade. My hope and ambition is that, between now and then, many of the unhealthy working practices that contribute to an imbalance in personal and professional lives are weeded out. That employees at all levels of the business from top to bottom and back again have a vested interest and personal stake in physical well-being and mental health. And that we don't have to explain that kindness is a strength not a weakness and is actually the smart choice.

If that inspires future generations to always come to work with joy, then I would have succeeded in honoring my father's approach. Through my work, it will have enabled and inspired others to continue his legacy and hopefully, in turn, begin to establish my own.

Bringing little moments of joy into every day can make all the difference to your people and your company.

So, let us all start with kindness.

It costs nothing and means everything. Especially to me.

This chapter is dedicated to my father, David Stevens, and to my son, Zack, and daughter, Ray.

Weaving a Web of Kindness

Beth Socoski

Beginning or continuing your personal kindness journey can take many paths. Some of us work on being kind to ourselves or others, some perform kind acts, and some want to learn more before acting.

Kindness is often portrayed as a ripple effect—drop a rock in the water, and watch the ripples travel outward. This is a great analogy, but I challenge you to think of it as a spider web—the rings of a web are connected, and every corner is intentionally connected to all other parts of the web. The ends of the web are attached to various points—a tree limb, a fence, a flower. If the web breaks at one point, it stays upright with its many connections. New connections can be woven, and repairs can be made if the web is damaged. At the very center is the hub, where the spider can often be seen.

Now, imagine that you are that spider.

You have bright, shining eyes; a soft, fuzzy belly; and a thread of silk. (Feel free to Google the term "cute spider" if you need a visual—or if you have a fear of spiders.) You (in cute spider form) sit on a tree branch. This branch is your home, your neighborhood. The other twigs and branches may be other neighborhoods or towns; the tree might be your city or another larger space.

You decide it is time to cast out your silk thread, with the goal of weaving a web. This may be the first and scariest moment for you. What if you reach for another branch and miss? What if the branch is broken or rotten inside and you didn't know? Reaching out is crucial to learning about what kind of web you might have, or how strong your tree is. At first, you need to make a small connection between your branch and a nearby smaller branch. A single silk thread is waiting to be cast.

Let's take a moment to talk about real spider webs. Part of the spiders' success as a species is because of its web. The web is their home, their protection from creatures that would cause harm, and how they find food. Spider webs are strong enough to carry the weight of the spider and its prey and withstand some threats (weather, the environment). They are flexible, and do not break in the breeze. Spiders use architectural instinct to change the type of silk used to create different parts of their web. Different kinds of spiders weave different styles of webs. As the little spider, you get to decide your web style, how flexible it will be, and how it best suits your kindness journey.

Though several branches may be nearby, picking the best one isn't always as important as just picking one and starting. If you have limited experience in community engagement, you may want to do research first. Think about what is important to you. It may be a long or short list, and there are no wrong answers for how you want to continue your kindness journey. Community engagement can open a doorway for many degrees of kindness.

First, determine what activities or organizations are a very strong "no" for you. This will help you immensely. Heavy lifting? Knocking on the doors of strangers? Religious affiliation? If an organization conflicts with your values, morals, and abilities, you should cross them off your list. It is normal to have moments of discomfort to help foster personal growth or understanding, but never compromise your beliefs—or even your personal safety! If you have a richer experience in community engagement, you have the luxury of your past experiences to help guide your decision-making.

What does this look like in real life? For me, it was living in a new city and deciding to volunteer. My company at the time had a robust volunteer listing, and I decided to sign up for a Saturday morning with Meals on Wheels, helping load volunteers' cars for a special program. It was a two-hour commitment—almost no time at all. I determined that, in the worst-case scenario, I would learn a little more about the neighborhood surrounding their building, explore an alternate route home, and get some physical exercise. This was me, cautiously swinging my first silk thread in the breeze.

Now, before your own thread meets the next branch, think about your intentions for community engagement. Why are you doing this activity? What will this activity bring to your kindness journey? The right intentions for engaging are vital to success. Think about a time when you were somewhere and did not want to be there. Perhaps it was a mandatory work/social event, a boring date, a family event that felt forced. You went through the motions of getting ready, putting on a happy face, perhaps even interacting a little. How did you feel after that forced interaction ended? Exhausted? Relieved? Irritated at the wasted time? Focus on that feeling for a few moments.

Community engagement centers on giving—you give your time, talents, and energy. That giving should never feel forced or uncomfortable. Rather, how do you *want* to feel when you commit and complete your community activity? Set your intentions to guide yourself to that desired outcome.

For my first engagement with Meals on Wheels, I decided that even if I disliked the activity or the organization, I was going to gain something from it—exercise, neighborhood geography, and knowledge about the organization. Anything additional that resulted from the experience, positive or negative, would be up to me to act upon.

I ended up loving it. A few other volunteers were from my company, and in two hours, we transitioned from random coworkers to friends with a mutual interest. The Meals on Wheels staff inspired me with their commitment and willingness to teach others about their amazing program. I met a lovely woman from France who volunteered every month with her beautiful teenage children and a local man who is one of the most positive people I've ever met (and he gives amazing hugs). More than two years later, we are still friends, and we check on each other if someone does not show up for our Saturdays with Meals on Wheels. We bring each other treats and books, and perform other kindnesses throughout the year.

This community engagement gave my nascent spider web a strong foundation—helping Meals on Wheels, helping the other volunteers deliver the Saturday packages, meeting other like-minded people in my company, and connecting with other people in my community. There is also the kindness to myself that occurred. The physical activity is a kindness to the body and mind. The social activity is a kindness to the emotional health. The relationship-building is a kindness to others.

Now the little spider has some threads touching other branches. That two-hour commitment, once a month, has built a small web—several silk threads are connected in many ways. People, places, and intentions are now all woven together. Each spot where two silk threads touch is a place where kindness has occurred.

In retrospect, I was lucky to have such a positive experience right out of the gate, as my experience could have been vastly different—I could have felt disconnected to the activity, not aligned with the organization's mission, physically unable to complete certain tasks, or pressured to do something I was uncomfortable with or could have had a personality conflict with someone. These are all very real and valid barriers to engaging successfully in your community. The kindness journey is not all sunshine and rainbows, and it may take a few attempts to find a community engagement activity that is right for you. There is nothing wrong with you or your intentions if an activity is a poor fit. A great part of being kind to yourself is knowing that you can say "no."

In the past, I was deeply involved with an organization focused on a specific disease, serving on their advisory committee, fundraising, performing advocacy work with politicians, and running a patient support group. Over the course of a year, their seasoned, committed staff began to leave or was downsized. The organization's mission changed, pulling focus away from the patients, and began to feel misaligned with my intentions. My fundraising dollars and hours spent trying to help patients were no longer having their intended impact, and I started to experience real conflict when I engaged with the organization. I decided to disengage. I struggled deeply with the decision, but I recognized that it was becoming a forced interaction, and my intentions were being compromised.

When something does not feel right or feels forced, you can disconnect that thread. This is often a kindness to yourself. While researching more about spiders, I learned the phrase "graceful failure." "Graceful failure" means that the design may fail, but the core function remains useable. A community engagement may be misrepresented, change over time as organizations adapt to change, or become misaligned with your principles as you continue on your kindness journey. Again, if you ever feel unsafe, take your web down, and move to another branch. Graceful failure is knowing that the web you are building has the right core function or intentions, but the current design may have some flaws. And that is perfectly normal.

What aspect of your community engagement experience helped you along your kindness journey? Allow yourself the time to recognize what made the experience positive for you and the organization, and review the actions that brought kindness to the community. Think about how your intentions were impacted by your activity—both positively and negatively. It is a kindness to yourself and the community when you can identify those factors and use them to make decisions. Evaluate what you can realistically add to your kindness journey. Overextending yourself is not a personal kindness, as this can eventually lead to burnout and a loss of positive connections.

I want to challenge that little spider to take the next steps in weaving the web. A strong, positive, community engagement experience is a solid foundation. You know what you like about what you are doing, how it makes you feel toward yourself and others, and how it spreads kindness in your community.

Thanks to the marvels of the internet, you can also weave your web in other ways. Remember the research you did before casting that first silk thread? You now get to share in someone else's discovery, as community engagement is alive and well online. Creating social media posts about the organization and its activities represents a great kindness to that organization. Sharing the organization with others helps widen *their* web, too. Your experience helps others in your community learn more about the organization, and helps others determine if they want to build their spider web there as well.

If you wish, you can increase your involvement with that organization, perhaps by volunteering more hours or taking on additional responsibilities. The organization may have an advisory group, a young leaders group, or a board that needs someone like you. All you have to do is ask.

Becoming involved with multiple organizations can allow you to utilize your many skills. At Meals on Wheels, I enjoy the physicality of the work and the visual progress that happens as cars are loaded. Combined with being outdoors, laughing frequently with the wonderful volunteers, and thanking every driver as they spread their own kindness by delivering, it is a joyful experience for me. At another organization, I serve on their board and use my wealth of earned knowledge to help shape and guide decisions that impact their services—plus the livelihoods of the employees. Being valued for your knowledge and abilities is deeply satisfying. Another organization, for which I am a board member, allows me to fill multiple roles—fundraiser, cheerleader, emcee, content creator, agenda pusher, and social butterfly. This can be a challenge at times, and I remember that I can always say "no" as an act of self-kindness, or ask for help from another volunteer.

Across the web you have woven, you can see all the people you now interact with as a result of your community engagement. Over time, you widen your professional and personal contacts as a result of your acts of kindness within the community. Friendships grow out of the seeds of mutual kindness. Your reach is now in their webs as well. You gain new skills, understand new perspectives, and better understand your own journey to self-kindness through these acts of community engagement.

Think of your own web now. From the hub, you can see where all your threads are anchored and where all the connections intersect. You have learned from any graceful failure, and know what silk works best for each situation. You can see where some threads need to be repaired, and others cut away—thus creating the opportunity for a new section to be built. You, cute little spider, get to be the architect of your kindness.

Be the spider.

Kindness from Ground Zero

Cori Wamsley

I asked my daughters what "kindness" means to them when I started writing this chapter. Talia, age 6, said it means, "Sharing and caring." London, age 8, said it means, "Nice and kind and lots of good stuff."

On the surface, yeah, they nailed it, but as I've been thinking about kindness lately, I realize that my grownup definition has so much more nuance. It's wrapped up in feelings and has boundaries, clearly delineating that it doesn't creep into obligation or expectation of something in return. It's something that I once thought I embraced, that I learned to be wary of, that I have now evolved into in a more empowered state of myself—what one of my colleagues calls the "Elite Empress"—that has allowed the deep warmth of a kindness performed or accepted to wash over me with love and gratitude.

But how does kindness get to be so complicated? How does it turn from friends sharing crackers on the back porch into a process that we may be wary or nervous about?

The Crooked Foundation

As a child, I remember learning about kindness in that false way where someone gives you a compliment because they want to be your partner on a project (because you get good grades). I came to associate it with the fair-weather friends of my school, the pretty girls who everyone liked. I quickly learned to withdraw and knew I was an ill fit at my school. I was harassed because my family didn't attend church (hello, sleeping in on Sundays!), and in the guise of kindness, friends and fake-friends alike would say that they thought I should go because they didn't want me to go to hell (already there!).

By middle school, I felt a thick wall forming around me to protect me from the false kindness. Yet, the funny thing about kindness is that we all have a desire for it deep down that nothing can quell. Feeling that most humans weren't going to be kind, I turned instead to the planet as a whole. I remember thinking about ways I could change the world. I decided that I would give to humanity (rather than specific people, because that was a painful thing) by working in a lab and curing diseases as an adult.

In the quiet space between classes and daydreaming of my grownup seclusion, I wrote. And the funny thing is that it was truly a kindness to myself to do so. I was an avid reader as a child and felt like writing a book would be a breeze (much like thinking that just because we can eat means that we can all be chefs). But that kindness to myself soon turned into "just play" as I looked at my skill in writing with a laugh. That's not a real job. That's a hobby. And I returned to the dream of working in a lab, silently, away from the people who were worth saving but not worth talking to.

As I grew up, I learned to treat myself with false kindness just as the kids in my elementary school had. I didn't take my true calling seriously and instead pushed toward the shoulds because money, accolades, and praise are major drivers and, though they may seem like kindness—and I think we are learning quickly that they need to be broached in a different way with those who are searching for their career—they can also become a list to check off, an unkindness that leaves us drying up inside, calling out for self-love and the warm embrace that we can only give ourselves through the kindness of listening to our deepest wishes.

Hollow

Of course, the farther we get from kindness to ourselves, the less able we are to give kindness to others. Judgement, instead, reigns as we look out onto what we believe to be a sick, sad world. Now, I know that it's all low-vibration crap that must be risen above, but in my 20s, I thought the planet was hurtling toward destruction guided by a bunch of heartless assholes because all I could see was the dark, dirty truths about humanity.

And when that becomes your lens, and you never pause to wonder if it just needs wiped off and the focus adjusted, you start to feel hopeless. I settled for a job that paid me barely enough to make it worth my while at a place where the bulk of the employees were bored, depressed, trying to figure out life, and looking for a hookup—and that could be a whole book in itself. I looked around and wondered if this was really adulthood, scraping by, cracking jokes about your sad life with your friends, and watching your marriage crumble because the other party had mentally checked out.

I had a moment with myself where I at least realized that a marriage where one of the partners spends every moment at home drinking and gaming wasn't worth keeping, and I was kind enough to myself to get out of it. It was a small step of kindness, but it at least let me see that if one thing wasn't working, maybe I didn't have to settle for the other pieces that weren't working either.

After detaching myself from that marriage, I also left that job, that house, and that state and moved to take what I thought would be a job that blended my talents and my love for the environment. As a science writer, I would be able to take kindness to a new level, showcasing the talented scientists and telling the world about the new technologies we were developing to mitigate carbon emissions from power plants and help the world have greener energy.

Kind to the world, yes. Kind to me, as I would soon find out, no.

Rising above the giant dumpster fire of my life, I thought the next chapter would be more kind, fun, and loving. I quickly made new friends who loved to go out salsa dancing, and I became a regular, two or three nights a week. That small kindness to myself let me explore my creativity because I've always loved dance. I paired that with writing novels during my spare time. But the drudgery of the day-job was soul crushing.

This time, there was no false kindness. There were certainly warm, wonderful people there, but their kindness was often overshadowed by the rude or flat out mean people I was exposed to. People complained about every little tiny thing like how I answered the phone or a slip-up in an article or the fact that my emails were "too businessy" and I should include more smileys and exclamation points so they knew I was happy. Seriously. Having grown up watching this pattern, focusing on the negative instead of the positive, I soon grew to expect this behavior.

Instead of embracing the previous hope and kindness that I felt when I leapt into that job, I now thought that the world truly was devoid of kindness. I cried myself to sleep often, dreading going back the next day. I looked forward only to seeing my friends and my new boyfriend and maybe someday figuring things out.

But I didn't prioritize being kind to myself, so I stayed there. I was too scared that another job would be worse. I was too scared that I would have to relearn people again. I already knew what I was dealing with at my job, so why risk worse?

But what if people elsewhere were kinder? The ripples of kindness certainly are as strong as the ripples of cruelty.

Instead of worrying about it, I plunged ahead with my personal life, getting married again, buying a house, taking two wonderful trips to Europe with my love, and having two beautiful little girls.

And though that sounds like a win, remember that there were always those boundaries with kindness, and now, I was building a household where I would be navigating them every day.

I wondered why my own husband would pick up my snack plate while I was working at my desk. I wondered why he decided to get up and change the baby before I nursed her at night. I wondered why he bought me something special for no reason. I stood firmly behind my walls, not understanding the kindness of those I loved most. I wasn't suspicious, but I was certainly perplexed.

There was no obligation. No malice. No kindness hiding something sinister. There was and still is just a man being kind because he loves a woman.

Thankfully, on my youngest daughters first birthday, something happened that turned out to be a huge wave of kindness from the Universe to me and my family. And this wave is something that has continued to give and give and give.

I lost my job.

The Spark of Kindness

On that day, I thought the world was ending, of course, but in truth, it was just beginning. Immediately after I lost my job in 2016, I started my writing coaching and editing business, and I started learning a lot about kindness, true kindness, and how it starts within.

Of course, the first thing I did when I found out that all the senior staff had been cut, which includes me, is cry, call my husband, and then post a rant about it on Facebook. But somehow, that negativity flipped on me. The kindness that poured out from friends and family was so touching. And I felt my heart soften a little, letting it in, fully accepting that this was for me, for no reason other than being kind.

Also, in kindness, a friend encouraged me to use my talents to start my own business. I had a small peek at what was to come from the entrepreneurial community.

In the five years that followed, I saw massive growth in myself and my brand, but only once I started embracing kindness at ground zero. It has to start within, and that was a huge, huge undertaking for someone who used to think that humans were innately cruel and bitter and gossipy—basically, judgmental mean girls without the cute outfits.

I had to embark on a journey of kindness toward myself, though I had no idea that this is what it actually was. I was a woman struggling with shitty self-esteem and two crazy, high-energy babies, one of whom wasn't even sleeping through the night. My husband was almost always at work in the evenings and on weekends, the times when I was most able to reflect on and, honestly, hate myself. I was tired, I *looked* like I had just given birth to two children, I wasn't eating as well as I thought I was, and I seriously wasn't sleeping. Throw in "figuring out a business" on top of that, and you have all the makings for a WTF sundae.

Fortunately, that old high-achiever fire somehow got lit because, thankfully, I have always had a fine-I'll-do-it-my-way attitude. Doing it my way meant that I got to recognize that "life on my terms" meant I didn't have to follow "the rules" anyway, so I started digging deep into how I actually wanted to live.

The scary thing is that somewhere between failed jobs and failed marriage, I lost my ability to dream. It wasn't safe in the world where dreams don't come true. That world wasn't kind to dreamers. They laughed at them. But when I seriously started asking, "What do I want?" I finally got back an answer other than "just surviving and paying the bills."

Other people's stories have always fascinated me. I love hearing about unique upbringings, faraway places, or stranger-than-fiction happenings. And when I stepped out into the entrepreneurial world, I soon discovered that people wanted to tell these stories.

Now here's the catch, when I first started hearing these stories, I thought that people wanted to use them to further their careers, to make money, to get attention. Yeah, that all may be true. But what is the REAL driver that will get people to admit to the most terrifying challenges, the steepest climbs, and the most breathtaking falls? The ugly parts? The shameful pieces? The drudgery of hitting rock bottom?

It's kindness. Truly. At heart, sharing your story is *kindness*.

Because people are sharing their stories to create an impact, to help others heal, to show them that there is better, that the sun will shine again.

They tell their stories as an act of kindness that can change the world.

This is where kindness and hope beautifully merge into a supernova and burst into a person's heart, letting them know that someone else succeeded, so they can too.

Humans have always been awed by stories. We have been mesmerized by cave drawings, by what the stars represent to early peoples, by the plays of ancient Greece and Rome, by poets, and bards, and novelists on into the modern era. And speakers, singers, sculptors, painters, dancers, and more tell stories, leading the audience to the edge of their seats and back again. Letting them see the unseen and feel more than they could ever hope to feel in a single lifetime.

Sharing our experience is kindness because it evokes feelings and soothes the soul. It is connection and trust and love.

And isn't that the best of the feeling of kindness that we want to spread around the world?

I attended a launch party for my author Sue Fattibene's first book *The Day the Angel Sat Beside Me* as I was working on this chapter, and in a conversation that evening, she summed it up perfectly, "I can't believe this is me, and I get to bless others with this."

As hard as it can be to own your story and actually write and publish it, it's that knowledge that your book can become the piece that gets someone else through their similar challenges that encourages you to push on and get it out there. It's a gift. It's kindness in tangible form.

Bringing it Home

As a mother, I never thought that I would have the privilege of guiding people to become authors and have my daughters by my side watching me do it. But I'm glad I get to do that.

The lessons that I have learned from the authors I work with have become part of my journey and part of my reach of kindness to the world.

It's a huge leap away from what I thought I would be doing as a teenager, and I wish I could go back and hug that girl and tell her to keep dreaming and don't worry about what people were telling her about wanting to design clothes or become an artist or write fantasy novels because the shift from listening to her heart to listening to what others thought was best for her was painful. Yes, she learned a lot, but I wonder how much faster I would have met my dreams if I hadn't brushed them aside and assumed that kindness from people who "knew better" was the best thing to guide me.

Being kind to myself over the past five years has meant a lot of changes. It means that I stopped listening to a doctor who told me at 18 that I should keep all the foods I'm allergic to in my diet so I wouldn't get sick if I accidentally eat them. Instantly feeling better is the reward I got for cutting them out and just saying "no" to cake at weddings or birthdays. It's made a world of difference in my mood, too.

I also realized that boundaries are kindness to myself; however, I don't need to block out the world. I need to find the right people to welcome into my space. I don't have to put up with people who bring me down, and it's kind to let go. It's kind to clear clutter from my house. It's kind to tell my kids that I'm not jumping up and down every time they yell "Mom." It's kind to focus on a dream of how my family wants to live and make changes to achieve it.

I appreciate that my daughters get to watch me do all this and learn from how I care for myself. I shudder to think about how many of my friends' moms when I was little were just shadows. They cooked, cleaned, drove the car, and flat out said that they were "living for their kids." I wonder what the world would be like today if someone had given them permission to be kind to and love themselves as much as their families.

In our house, my children meditate with me. We watch movies and read the books we love. We talk about our dreams and how we can make a difference in the world.

As someone who was often laughed at for saying that I was writing novels and wanted to get them published, I'm much kinder with my kids' dreams. I don't expect the world to tell them that becoming a mermaid when they grow up is feasible, but I am teaching them to ask, "How can we make that happen?"

The bigger lesson that I hope my children see from my rebellious turn toward kindness is that I work with change-makers and world-shakers who were kind enough to know that their story isn't just for them. I want them to understand that you don't have to donate to every organization and cause that comes your way. You don't have to crush your dreams and accept what someone else wants of you. And you don't have to sacrifice your body, your mind, and your soul as a mother to serve your family or create happiness for them.

Kindness to yourself always ripples out. And my girls will grow up to see that they are the most important people in their lives, and that by owning this, they can then be kind in whatever direction their hearts lead them.

So how can you be kind to yourself?

1) **Hustle hurts.** When you are rushing around, trying to put everyone and everything first, you have to put you last. This means that you aren't going to watch as much for things that you need, desire, crave. It means that you are pushing kindness to yourself aside in an effort to be kind to others,

and that's not kindness. That's obligation and lack of boundaries.

2) **Prioritize love.** Sometimes kindness is a hard truth. If it feels like it sucks, then maybe it's still kindness because it's love. Maybe you need to cut out a relationship, a food, a bad habit, but in the end, you are being kind to yourself and your truth.

3) **Listen to your heart.** And your gut. This is the biggest lesson I had to learn about kindness. I thought I was being kind to others when I responded to every email and Facebook message because I didn't want them to feel like they were being ignored, but I was also blocking my intuition by pushing through that "gut feeling" that said, "Don't talk to that person. Don't engage. Don't let this go further." Letting your body tell you if something feels ok and deciding if it's a good scared (like pushing your comfort zone for a good, growing outcome) or a bad scared (like this is a bad decision and I shouldn't do it) is so important. Today, if I feel that little tightness in my gut, I know that something is up. My body knows, which means I know, which means I can adjust my course. Always trust your inner wisdom to lead you to kindness.

I asked my daughters about how kindness feels in their bodies when they experience true kindness (not the fake kind), and they agreed that they feel warmth in their hearts, and it impacts their whole day.

I hope that you, too, can feel that warmth in your heart as you choose to be kind to yourself and other people and causes that you champion. And I hope that the warmth kindles a fire that stretches around the entire planet, creating a more caring, loving place to call "home."

Living Kindly

Kindness is Badass.

Jo Davis

Kindness does not have to be warm, fuzzy, and pink. In my own life and working with hundreds of clients, I have discovered that kindness can be just the opposite. It can be messy, imperfect, and brave. It is not caring who is watching, what the neighbors think, or if people like you for your big heart or not. That is, frankly, none of your business. Most often, the less you care what others think, the more pure the gesture. Whether they appreciate or are grateful for the act of kindness is, again, not your business.

The more courageous you are in taking action, the more significant the difference you can make in the lives around you and, ultimately, the world. It is the energy and unattached intention behind the action that will change a life. That means you do the right thing for the right reason. If it is kind, you do it. Period. You are unattached to the gratitude or praise from the world around you. It is through the higher calling of LOVE that you choose to live your life. This was my hard lesson in the meaning of "badass kindness."

After losing my great six-figure corporate job and most of the friends that I had worked with for nearly a decade, I began to dissect the "kindness quotient" in my life. How much of who I am in actions and words is kind, caring, generous? You would think that, if so many of my employees and coworkers went silent and disappeared from my life at the end of my corporate career, I must have been a wretched boss! I would instantly think that if you were telling me this story. However, this was not the case. There is much more to this story and my lessons in the meaning of kindness.

While I agree that we should all be mindfully attentive to our inner and outer work, aside from all the warm fuzzy practices of generosity, I ask that we dig deeper in this conversation. Paying for the car behind you in the drive-thru is wonderful, as long as you know why you are doing it. In this chapter, we will get a little bit more real and raw about the most important aspect of kindness that no one is talking about. The gritty side of kindness. The place where the Universe rewards your authenticity and unabashed generosity with deep, authentic relationships, abundance, and good health. That was what I was missing in my life. And that starts with badass kindness.

We are born naturally loving, generous creatures: chubby faces and rosy cheeks. Arms outstretched and hearts open. We are born with the deep desire to love others coursing through our veins. We want to hold others and be held. We want to make others smile and laugh. Piling our toys on mom's or dad's lap, sharing juice boxes, our Legos, our dolls, and treats feels good. Giving brings us joy. Little moments of giving fill our day as toddlers, and at our essence, we are saying, "I see you. I like you. I love you." There is no judgment, no expectation, and no keeping score.

Have you ever watched a toddler play with their friends on a summer day? Setting up the teacups, plates, and pretend food. As friends sit around the table, they pass around the food and make sure that things are mostly fair. One of the children will take charge; another is happy to be a helper. The others are content to sit at the table and play together. It is not complicated. Children wish for joy in every single experience. They do what feels good in their heart. Each moment is met with curiosity and a need for pleasure. They do not see strangers. They see friends. They do not see race or color, and they are not bound by beliefs. They feel and do. It is that basic.

As a child, this behavior feels effortless because it is who we are at our core. We have basic needs that need to be filled, and our response to having our needs filled is uncomplicated.

Then we grow up. In the home, gathering for dinner, we may hear our parents exchanging stories about their workday. We listen to them discussing conflict and, on occasion, venting. Talking about their coworkers, employees, or boss, saying things like," I expect others to treat me with the same respect I treat them." We begin to learn the requirements and demands of interpersonal relationships. The playbook for how the world works is laid out for us—revealing itself as we eavesdrop on adult conversations. That dance of giving and receiving gets muddy. The scorecard overshadows that natural ability to be kind.

Eventually, we find ourselves in relationships, navigating fulfilling our needs and those needs of the ones we love. Adulting is complex. There are so many moving parts—tasks and a to-do list that go on for days. Our lives are woven into careers and bills, often including a family. It's all a juggling act of what requires our attention that day. Our parents' words echo in our heads, the rules of engagement in the world, "I expect others to treat me with the same respect I treat them." That shifts into relationships where now our behavior is a tool.

We act in specific ways TO BE LOVED and accepted. We are kind and generous BECAUSE we wait on the receiving end to be rewarded for our efforts. That is what we expect. I am behaving this way and crossing my fingers that in filling your love bank, you will fill mine as well. That reward could be time, energy, or affection from those in our daily lives. We strive for this reward. We are constantly doing and giving and bleeding out our energy for all the wrong reasons. We write stories of our selflessness and collect people along the way that we believe will sing our praises.

Where does kindness fit into this new expectation?

Kindness begins to take special effort in this fast-moving, grown-up world. It becomes a smaller piece of our identity than when we were toddlers playing in the yard, taking turns running through the sprinklers and making sure that our mom invited every single kid on the block to our birthday party to share in the fun. Once, kindness was our entire being; our essence now presents itself as a rare occurrence in everyday life. It is such a unique way of being as adults that we begin to celebrate it as a big deal. News stations create a weekly kindness corner. We are sharing stories of generosity and everyday heroes. Newspapers and social media outlets jump on board as well.

How do we snap out of this adult space of holding back and dive unabashedly into that childlike space of generosity? It takes a wake-up call, a smack down, a tragedy, a lesson in authenticity.

We have all experienced a season in our lives that you might call the "striving to be better" season. Some might call it their way of life—constantly growing and evolving. It is a beautiful thing to have the desire to do better. I had spent upwards of twenty years doing just that. I was reading, studying, growing, and being kind, and making kindness towards others my purpose. I strove to be the people in those hero stories. I took every opportunity to do what I believed was the kind thing. However, my life was not a reflection of that. I was a hot mess. I was jobless, confused, and heartbroken. So, what was I doing wrong? What was I missing?

The journey of personal growth and development is a moving target. I strongly encourage anyone reading this who can relate to my story to give yourself some grace. Do not beat yourself up. Life is challenging. It is getting on and off the different train cars, shifting into different seasons of our life and jumping onto the other lines leading to new destinations. The train car that we ride during our first marriage, switching onto another train car in a new career path, then hopping onto a new rail line raising kids. All while learning, all while navigating the many souls that cross our way as we live our lives striving to be more decent humans. Or, for the overachievers reading this book, becoming a super-kind kind of human. We in our hot mess of lessons, and them in theirs. It is not always pretty, and frankly, it often looks like a sitcom of characters coming and going on the stage before us. I loved the stage analogy as I picked up my bucket of popcorn and glass of wine to examine my own personal shit-show at the age of forty-two.

Taking a step back from our lives and reflecting is the most valuable gift we can give ourselves. In that impersonal, slightly disconnected space, we can get honest and come clean about why we do what we do.

Growing up in a strict religious household, I was always striving to prove my goodness. My worthiness was wrapped up in doing enough and being enough to everyone and anyone. The act of being kind was to earn some sort of ranking, family acceptance, community admiration, getting into Heaven, etc. You get the point.

I was raised by a mother who took pride in the sacrifices she made, reminding us daily how she went without providing for us. To my impressionable eyes, that is what love was. The "struggle" was love. Giving was not effortless, and you wore it like a badge of honor. It was easy for me to slide into the dynamics of our home. I was a people pleaser. I was naturally a helper, a giver, a doer for others. See a need. Fill a need. I was good at it. As a child, I was publicly praised for it. I believed that this was my authentic self. I was the peacemaker, the fixer, the soft place for everyone to land. So, I became an expert at showing up in support of other's lives. I lifted others up and gave until I had little left for myself. I had the rolling *Rocky* theme song looping in my head and imagined pulling out my superhero cape and tights when the task called for that extra-extra mojo.

I had accumulated years of volunteer work in nursing homes, animal shelters, and adopting and fostering animals. I was the lifetime designated driver for every gathering and was always prepared with extra snacks, drinks, supplies for any occasion. I had donated art, time, money to fundraisers and nonprofits. I even went so far as to quit a job to sit with a family friend who had suffered a stroke. And plasma? I had donated so much plasma that they told me to stop coming to donate!

The resume for my Mother Theresa application was extensive, and I was pretty proud of my selflessness.

I had mastered achieving external validation. I sweat "goodness," and my karma bank must be overflowing at this point. I was a GOOD HUMAN. Indeed, my golden ticket to Heaven was in the mail. My halo was soon to return from the shop, all shiny and repaired. Shouldn't my life feel whole by now? Peace in my heart? Joy billowing over me, carrying me through all my struggles? Right?

No.

My life was out of balance, in disarray. For as much as I desperately wanted to be seen, I felt invisible. There was nothing special about me or the person I had become. I was surrounded by people for whom I had filled a need, and they were, of course, more than happy to continue showing up to be loved on and cared for. Sadly, I was empty and lost. Everything felt hard. I was tired and I felt insignificance in the world. I had bled out for people who were quick to move on to the next refill station to get their needs met when I closed up shop. That was eye-opening.

I was raised to see acts of kindness as behavior that led to an end. A destination. A box you check to achieve goodness. It was always spun in a web of expectations and, ultimately, disappointment.

This was a turning point. As I sat in my office that cool September morning, boxing up ten years of my life, my personal belongings, it felt surreal. Trying to choke back the tears as my insides rattled and my heart was racing. I knew that this was all MY lesson. The woman that wanted my job was not the problem. The company cutting costs was not the problem. The pain in my heart was mine. All my doing. Those emotions needed some examination. As much as it hurt, I knew that I had gotten myself to this place, and I was the only one who could ensure that it did not happen again.

Like Sisyphus, I was pushing that boulder up the mountain day in and day out. I had gotten stuck in this cycle. I was repeating this hardwired loop of proving my worthiness, of being a good person, and being kind enough.

As I sat alone in my house staring at boxes of memories, pictures of work trips and parties, and knickknacks, I remembered a coworker. Someone who I considered a friend. She had left a toxic relationship and moved into a one-bedroom apartment with barely the clothes on her back. Within two weeks, I had found her every essential supply she needed through a variety of resources. A bed, curtains, kitchen table, art, you name it. I got it handled. After I departed from my job, she disappeared from my life, as did nearly every one of my coworkers.

The many stories of my good deeds felt like daggers in my heart. They brought me no comfort because I had no idea who I was or *why* I was doing these things. This revelation took the air from my lungs and brought me to my knees. "Kindness" was a word that, on that day, felt bristly and stung. It brought on feelings of resentment and anger. Oddly, these were the first real honest emotions I had felt in years. Yes, it felt a little dark, but it also felt clean and authentic. It felt refreshing, like a glimmer of hope. It was a slice of the real me, my most beautiful imperfect self, peeking out. My heart was longing for this version of myself. In that split second, that messy space felt more like home than the previous twenty years of my life. My grandmother taught me, "If everyone looked out for everyone, everyone would have everything they need." It was a beautiful sentiment, but there was no talk of self-love or balance.

There was no teaching that, "You have nothing to prove!" It was time to start digging deep and asking myself the hard questions.

Was I being kind? Or was I selfish in my acts of kindness? This was the beginning of my road to badass kindness, joy, peace, and an abundance of heart-centered experiences and relationships in my life.

How could loving and giving and doing for others leave me feeling so empty? *Because expectation and attachment are the root of all suffering.* It was that simple. This did not require a yearlong stay at a Buddhist Temple to find myself or a 30-day silent meditation in Costa Rica. It did not happen through an Ayahuasca ceremony in Peru, exploring my inner shadows. I did not need to read another hundred books or attend more spiritual retreats led by our time's most enlightened spiritual thought leaders. I just looked in the mirror and started asking the questions, starting with "Who are you at your core?"

We can look at the dynamics of a toddler interacting with the world and recognize that they are fluid in that space of love and joy. They move through every interaction with impulsivity and clumsiness. They are not weighing out how the world sees them or calculating how their behavior lands on an adult scorecard or balance sheet. Playing and laughter feel good. Kindness feels good to receive and give. They are drawn to it and push and demand for more. I am no different. At my core, I crave it ALL TOO.

How do acts of kindness come naturally and feel good? "Effortless" is the word that rings in my ears as I type this. The way a child breathes love into a home is effortless. The smiles, piling their toys on your lap, passing out candy, and pretending to fill their friends' teacups. We are innately wired to be kind. It is in our DNA. It is until we begin to care about what the world thinks. The joy in these experiences is so powerful that I can feel it in every cell of my body when I immerse myself in it. I know that it is healing me. I move through challenging days more quickly when I am in that high frequency. When I am sad or struggling? I always feel better loving on others, being generous with honest compliments, and sharing what I have in time or money.

Why do you care what the world thinks about you?

Ultimately, this question took 20 years of my good deeds and brought to light the ugly truth. Though most often it felt good to give, my intention behind the act was always self-serving. My religious upbringing, my need to be accepted and liked, and my deepest desire for a high-vibe-girl tribe of friends who loved me was all at the root of this painful season of my life. I did to receive. Nothing I longed for manifested in this muddy place of "doing to receive." My expectations of the world around me negated my efforts. The Law of Attraction was just dishing out more lessons because I never showed up for the right reasons. There was nothing kind in my intentions. My choices were all filled with attachment to acceptance. I was driven by my need to earn my place in the world as a good person, all calculated and based on my adult scorecard.

I lacked the courage to be my authentic self, be disliked, and be thought of as weird or different. I would never show up clumsy and awkward and fill a need because it was the right thing to do. I only showed up well put together and for the accolades. It was such a habit that I did not even realize I was doing it. I was on autopilot. This part of me was so stealth that most would have never drawn this conclusion. I subconsciously weighed out my actions on the balance sheet—the scale of what I desired and how my actions would manifest that desire. I was unhappy. I was exhausted. All because I was not true to my core, my soul.

The ugly cry is the final stopping point for me in this story. I was alone in my living room on day three in my fuzzy pj's. At that moment, I decided what kindness would look like for me. It would look raw, honest, and unabashed. I would no longer care what the world thought of my random acts of kindness or who was grateful. I would give and do because it felt amazing. I would be fierce and silly and no longer expect any validation for showing up to do the right thing. If the world misunderstood my generosity in words or actions, it was not my concern. It was not my business. Crumpled in a pile on my living room floor, face puffy, and needing a shower, a stillness came over me. My mind became quiet and my heart felt full. I felt more alive than I had felt in years discovering and owning my truth.

When we spin our worthiness, our ego, our needs, and desires into the act of loving others, the Universe sees our B.S. It is not a truth that you can hide under an expensive business suit, red lipstick, and good hair. The truth is the truth.

Since that day, my life has completely changed. The courage to be kind without any expectations has positively affected every aspect of my life. It has propelled me to harness my gifts as an intuitive, becoming a published author, a teacher, and a public speaker and, ultimately, to create Lift A Sister Up, an organization to support and shine a light on the incredible power of women supporting women in life and business. I began manifesting the most amazing opportunities and deeply grounded friendships. Badass kindness is our superpower. It is liberating and will free you from unnecessary pain and disappointment.

If you choose to embrace "the act of being kind as the right thing to do regardless of the world watching," it will change the trajectory of your life because deciding to be kind is what your soul craves. When you let go of how the world sees you and throw yourself into what brings you joy in the act of serving others, you will manifest an epic life. You will change, and the world will change around you.

The $10 Kindness Club: Making Change with a Few Dollars

Francesca Donlan

I teach a kindness class at Florida Gulf Coast University in Fort Myers, Fla.

The class fills with students who want to understand kindness and how it can change them and the world at the same time—it's called "The Kindness Effect."

Kindness can be taught, which is the first thing you should know. Science and research continue to demonstrate that kindness is critical to our success as human beings. And right now, the United States is suffering a kindness deficit.

The students who enroll in my kindness class don't arrive with hardened hearts looking to be kinder. Many want to strengthen their kindness muscles and make a difference.

Some of these students haven't seen much kindness and want to see it first-hand.

Some have been manipulated by kindness.

Some have been blessed with kindness and want to pay it forward.

Some understand kindness but aren't very kind to themselves.

They all want to live in a kinder world.

We study the science and research around kindness and discuss the social, physical, psychological, and economic benefits of kindness. We also do a variety of kindness challenges, which often push the students out of their comfort zone.

One of those assignments is the $10 Kindness Challenge.

In the past, I felt like philanthropy belonged to the rich. And that type of thinking prevented me from giving what I could with what I had. But philanthropy comes in many forms, and I wanted to empower my students to make a difference in the ways that they could.

So, I thought I would see what kind of magic we could create with $10. I asked a friend, Sharon Arnold, if she would become our "kindness patron." If artists can have patrons, why can't kindness students? For the past three semesters, Sharon has given $10 to each student in the class. They have two weeks to spend it on someone in need. They can spend it in any way they wish, as long as it involves an interaction. They can't donate anonymously. First, I advise them to carry it with them and see if something comes up naturally the first week. If not, they should have a Plan B and spend the money the next week. They also have to present how they spent the money to the class and write a paper about it, which includes three research elements that illustrate why giving is important.

Some wonder if the money would be more impactful if it came from the student's own pocket. But research says "no." It also says giving away just a little bit of money has the same effect on happiness as giving away a lot, according to Philippe Tobler, associate professor of neuroeconomics and social neuroscience from the University of Zurich in Switzerland.

Tobler conducted a study where he gave participants $100 and asked half to spend it on themselves and half to spend it on someone they knew.

Those who gave the money away reported higher levels of happiness. Tobler concluded that being generous can increase well-being and happiness.

And after watching almost 100 students participate in the $10 Kindness Challenge, I can attest that it doesn't matter where the money came from. The results and experiences have been so powerful that the giving is both beneficial to the giver and the recipient.

I have never looked at $10 the same since I started this challenge.

Some of the experiences my students have had giving away $10 may convince you to join the $10 Kindness Challenge—I hope so.

Inspiration and Ice Cream

Wiktoria Czarnecka arrived at Florida Gulf Coast University as a freshman and member of the college swim team. She came all the way from Poland to realize her dream.

She had been in Fort Myers for two weeks when she decided to go to Publix and buy some ice cream to help combat homesickness. It had been a tough transition—a new country with no friends or family. But as she swiped her credit card, it declined. She swiped it again and again and grew more and more flustered. All of a sudden, a woman behind her in line reached forward with her credit card.

"Don't worry," the stranger said. "I got you."

And that experience made Wiktoria finally feel at home in the community. It gave her an enormous lift. When it was time to spend her $10, she went to Publix and paid for someone else in line.

"It turned out to be a lady," Wiktoria said about the woman she chose to give $10. "And she was very caught off guard and overwhelmed, but also grateful and excited about it. The part where I gave the money for the groceries felt so good and rewarding. I decided to always remember about doing something unexpected and nice in the future. It felt like I was on such a high because of doing something good for others."

Holiday Ready

Guadalupe Duran-Almaras always escorted her best friend to a local grave site to decorate his grandmother's grave. They pulled the weeds, bought flowers and added decorations if they were there near a holiday. Guadalupe joined her friend at the gravesite—this time to decorate for Christmas. Guadalupe looked around and noticed that neighboring graves didn't have flowers or decorations.

"There were other pretty graves, very well kept with nice little gifts," she said. "There were also a lot of lonely graves."

She was going to spend that Christmas with her father and felt a little lonely, and she "didn't want the dead to feel like I do."

"Sometimes people get busy, or they move, or maybe it's too hard for them to go visit their loved ones. I decided since I had time that day, and an extra $10 dollars, we'd go decorate them," she said.

They bought packs of holiday bows.

"We drove back to talk to them and put a bow on for the holidays. It was nice, I personally enjoyed it. I hope they did too. They're all ready for the holiday season now! Hope they feel appreciated and respected."

Crafty Generosity

Emma Goldman shared a love of crafting with her grandmothers. But when one of her grandmothers began to suffer from dementia and moved to a memory care facility, they couldn't craft like they did in the past. So, she found a way to use her $10 to honor one grandmother and help the other grandmother remember.

She went to Goodwill and bought vases. She went to a craft store and purchased silk flowers, ribbon and tissue paper. She went home and printed out photos of herself. She glued the photos around each vase brimming with of silk flowers.

"Since one of my grandmas lives in a memory care facility and has dementia, seeing those pictures on a vase next to flowers will hopefully remind her of me and make her as happy as I am feeling at the thought of even giving them these gifts," Emma said.

Coffee Break

Savannah Daniel found solace at the Starbuck's drive-through. Sometimes, she would drive to Starbuck's when she felt sad to cheer herself up. But one day, with $10 in her pocket, she found a moment to cheer someone else up.

"On a day when I was feeling fine and just going to get coffee, no tears in my car," she said. "I was ordering my drink when I could see in my rearview mirror the girl behind me was crying. It looked like she was on the phone, and I didn't know what she was crying over, but it looked like she was having a bad day. I could completely see myself and all the times I have come through the same drive-through line crying, and in that moment, I just wished there was something I could do to make her feel better. When I paid for my coffee, I also paid for whatever she had gotten. I hope it made her feel even a tiny bit better on her rough day, and she could know someone cared."

A few minutes later, they pulled up at the same light and waved to each other.

Kinkajous and Kindness

Nick Drummond has a mad love for animals. He works as a zookeeper at a local nature park and consistently comes to class and shares a new scratch or bite from the animals that he loves so much.

He decided to use his $10 for enrichment toys for the animals. He went to a local thrift store and got $10 worth of supplies. He stuffed Wiffleballs with bananas and cantaloupe for the tree weasel or the coatimundis (an animal like a raccoon). He filled a Nerf football with treats for the South American kinkajou and froze it like a popsicle. He rolled toilet paper cores in peanut butter and bird seed for the parrots. He filmed a video so the class could see all the animals having fun with the toys.

"It was not only good for the animals, but it was good for me because it gave me a hobby to do and think of, which in turn, improved my mental health," he said. "Be kind to animals. They will love you back."

Special Delivery

Stormy-Dawn Lambert was eagerly waiting for a package from Amazon when she got the notification that it had been delivered. She went to get her package and realized it was not addressed to her. It felt like it may have been medicine, and she wanted to deliver it to the owner.

The package belonged to a woman in a neighboring apartment. She knocked on the neighbor's door.

"When the door opened, I was surprised to see an older woman in her 80s maybe, still in her pajamas, and the smell that came out of her apartment smelled like my grandmother's house," she said.

"I learned that she lived alone, and her husband had passed away a few years prior and she didn't have family in the area. She also didn't drive or get out much. She reminded me a lot of my own grandmother, and I thought about how difficult it must be to be alone."

Stormy chose to spend her $10 buying her neighbor a box of brownies and a pizza. Then she asked her if she could join her as well.

"I try to stop by and say 'hello' to her once a week," she said. "No one deserves to be all alone in this world, and I think it takes a hard toll on our bodies to essentially live in isolation for so long. I think about my own grandmother, who has severe dementia. I wish I was able to just sit and talk with her, but unfortunately, it's just not possible anymore. I don't think she truly knows how much I get out of our interactions either. I hope that I can continue to see her and check in on her so she knows she's not all alone anymore."

A Wave of Kindness

Ariandne Vasquez lived in a low-income housing community. Every morning as she left for college with her backpack slung over her shoulder, an elderly man sitting outside the complex would wave "hello." One morning as she left for class, she saw him again and was reminded of all the times he had been so silently kind to her. She decided to give him the $10.

She tentatively approached him for the first time. They had never spoken before. But she gathered her courage and told him that she would like to give him $10 for lunch.

He would not take the money.

"I was taken aback," she said. "I kept insisting to him that I just want to show him the same kindness that he had shown me every time I make my way to class. And he said, 'Well then keep going to class and finish. I don't need this money, but thank you.' And here I am just with $10 in my hand unsure of what to do because I thought handing someone the money would be the easiest part."

She wished him a great day and drove to class with the $10 still in her pocket. But the experience moved her to tears.

"This old man taught me such a valuable lesson about how easy it is just to be nice," she said. "We think if we had all the money in the world that we could save everyone but that's not the case here. Being nice is a way of showing a great example of what it means to be a human being. To this day I have no idea who that old man is [. .] but, in my eyes, I see him as a sign of hope. Hope that humanity still has people who are kind in this world. After dealing with so many not so nice people at this point in my life, it's hard to be nice again. But it feels just as refreshing when a stranger can put that faith back in your heart. So, I just wanted to thank Francesca and to thank our patron for such an opportunity because what I thought was going to be an easy assignment turned out to be an epiphany for me. Kindness is a way of spreading hope of a new future, and I only wish I had this class sooner."

More Kindness Challenges

And there are so many more stories. Dillon Long gave $10 to a boy at Barnes & Noble who wanted to read about kid athletes. Dillon loves to read and was so happy to see a young person at a bookstore without an electronic device. Students Caitlyn Sapka, Vanessa Miguel, and Skylar Allen used T-shirts they bought at a thrift story to create dog toys.

Edward Hanna turned his $10 into quarters to pay for student laundry. It cost $1 per dryer cycle. One student wasn't going to do all of her laundry that day but could after getting an extra dollar from Edward. Keelin Hoffman flew to Dallas for a conference. The Florida native forgot to bring warm clothes for her February trip. It was 30 degrees when she landed. She went to a department store to buy a coat and saw a homeless man sitting outside with no shoes. She asked for his shoe size and bought him a pair of boots and some socks. Brianna Marchel spent $10 dollars on chalk and other toys to hand out at a park in a low-income area. Alexander Hussey remembered a middle school teacher who gave all the students mints before a big test. But Alex never ate his because he didn't like mints. The teacher noticed and gave Alex a grape Jolly Rancher instead. It meant a lot to Alex that his teacher cared that much. Alex used part of his $10 to thank that middle school teacher with a big bag of grape Jolly Ranchers.

These $10 challenges continue to surprise and delight me. The students have direct experiences with philanthropy and have realized they can make change. There is so much we can do to be kind. It just takes time and imagination. I learned through the big hearts of my students that kindness can have a profound impact no matter how much money you have.

$10 Kindness Club: I started a group on Facebook in the summer of 2020: @10kindnessclub. It's a small but mighty group that inspires and encourages each other to make a difference. Please join us there, and help us spread more kindness.

Living Kindly

Billy Refused the Call: A Story of Kindness at Work

Magnus Wood

Billy refused the call.

Here it was again, "No Caller ID," which was appearing on his cellphone with increasing frequency. He never picked up calls he didn't recognize the number for and certainly ones where the number wasn't displayed. Probably just trying to sell him something he didn't need or want.

He flipped his phone over, pushing this unwelcome intrusion away so he could return to thinking about work.

Things were not going well at work.

Actually, that was a complete understatement.

Things were going terribly.

Every morning when Billy woke up, his first thought was that he wished he hadn't. His second, third, fourth, and countless other thoughts, as he lay there not wanting to move, were all negative. Thoughts of the horrible day he had yesterday and the day before. Thoughts of what he knew was coming up today. Thoughts of what he feared might happen. These thoughts were coming at him faster and faster, and his nerves jangled with the early warning signs of yet another panic attack.

That spurred Billy into action, and he hauled himself out of bed.

He showered, then made himself a strong espresso, and picked up his phone to check his work emails and messages.

And there it was again. "No Caller ID." "This guy sure is persistent," he thought as he pressed the "Decline" button to refuse the call.

Ten minutes later, Billy was out the door, wound up by the emails that had come in overnight once he'd fallen asleep on his sofa after chugging half a bottle of wine in front of the television.

It was 7:10am. His day had not started well. And it definitely wasn't going to end well.

Just like every day at work.

~~~

Most of us will work for 50 years, and we spend, on average, a quarter of our adult lives at work. That's 13 years. 4,821 days. The only thing we do more of? Sleep. In our lives we spend, on average, 26 years asleep. We spend more time at work than doing the things we really enjoy, 12 hours working for every hour spent socializing, for example. Work dominates our time, our emotions, our energy . . . our whole lives.[1]

And yet work makes us miserable and unwell. 85% of the world's workers are unhappy at work.[2] Work should be a source of joy, but in fact, it is making more and more of us physically and mentally ill—and it is happening at an increasing rate too.[3]

153,424 of us die every day. That's 106 people every minute.[4]

Let's be generous and say that only half of these people work for a living.

85% of 53 is 45.

That's 45 people every minute dying without knowing the joy of work they love. Worse than that—they died having spent a quarter of their adult lives doing work they didn't enjoy, work that didn't fulfil them. All just to earn money for lives they didn't love.

Every day, work can give you some of your greatest joy. Joy that gives you meaning and purpose. Joy that makes you excited when you wake up in the morning. Joy that lights up all of your life.

---

[1] https://www.dreams.co.uk/sleep-matters-club/your-life-in-numbers-infographic/

[2] https://www.gallup.com/workplace/285674/improve-employee-engagement-workplace.aspx

[3] https://www.cipd.co.uk/about/media/press/good-word-index-2020

[4] https://www.medindia.net/patients/calculators/world-death-clock.asp

But in the time it has taken you to read this section, 45 people have died without having fulfilled their true potential or experienced some of their deepest joys through work.

Work made them miserable. Work made them physically and mentally ill. Just like it was doing to Billy . . .

~~~

"You're a hard man to pin down."

Billy looked up from his drink at the individual approaching him at the bar and felt a flicker of recognition. He knew this guy, but he couldn't quite place him.

"Hello, Billy. Remember me?"

A few hours and a few drinks later, they were looking at photos on George's phone. Photos of a group of smiling twenty-somethings standing at a water pump, along with what appeared to be the inhabitants of an entire village wearing their finest traditional tribal outfits.

It had been a big day—the completion of a pump that brought water to this Kenyan village for the first time. Billy and George were volunteers in their gap year before university. They had been good friends then but had lost touch over the years. Last he'd heard, George was working for his father's construction company.

"What happened to us, George? All those good intentions. We were going to change the world."

"You mean you haven't?" George was smiling, but Billy could see that something else was on his mind.

"We were dreamers then, my friend. Yes, I wanted to change the world but my student loan, and rent, and car payments, and saving for a house deposit . . . they all took over."

"So, is that why you're stuck in a job you hate?"

"And you're not?"

"No. I'm not. I'm lucky, but I also made my own luck. My father passed away six months ago—"

"I'm sorry to hear that."

"Thanks. But we weren't so sad in the end because it had been coming for a while and he'd had a chance to get his things in order, make peace with himself and the people he loved. In fact, he was able to spend the last six months of his life being truly kind."

~~~

Kindness.

Together in this book we're exploring, encouraging, and celebrating kindness.

What "Living Kindly" means. How it makes people feel. And its power to change the world.

And what better place to be kind than where we spend a quarter of our lives? A place that makes 85% of us unhappy.

Work.

Kindness at work.

Those three little words...

Chances are you won't have seen them together much. Only 124,000 results when I have just googled "kindness at work." And that compares with the 3,530,000 when I searched "stress at work." There's something deeply wrong here.

You have this book in your hands. You must believe in the power of kindness. The power of kindness to create work with meaning and joy that make the world a richer place.

Billy believed in that once. But then he refused the call . . .

~~~

"So, what are you doing here anyway? You don't even live round here."

"I came to see you. I kept calling you, but you never picked up. And what I have to say I couldn't tell you by text."

They were a few drinks in, having caught up on each other's lives. Billy was doing a job he didn't enjoy—the latest in a long and depressing CV of jobs like that. George commiserated with him. But what he didn't say was that his old friend was looking worn out, and it was a sure bet that the scruffy athleisure clothes he was wearing had never seen the inside of a gym.

George's father's passing was bittersweet. George loved his old man deeply and was still coming to terms with the fact that he would never chat with him again or see him around the place. But one of his father's last acts was to sell the business, which had left George, an only child whose mother had died five years ago, with choices. The money was only one part of his father's legacy. The other element—the kindness—would be revealed soon enough . . .

"Your father always had time for everybody. It's one of the things I remember most about him."

"Yes, Dad was kind. But he wasn't just kind when he'd made a success of himself. He was kind all his life, even when we first lived in a trailer, and right until his last day. Dad said being kind made everybody's lives richer. He genuinely believed that's how the world worked. And judging by what he built, the number of people who came to his funeral, and what people had to say about him, I know that being kind worked for Dad."

"He was very good to me. I remember he always had time to listen and give advice."

"Do you remember any of it?" George looked intently at Billy. This wasn't a casual question. There was real purpose behind it.

"Do you remember any of the advice my father gave you?"

~~~

We're generally not very good at seeing the consequences of our decisions and actions.

That little extra portion or that drink you didn't need? It doesn't amount to much . . . until one day you realize that most of your clothes don't fit and you're spending all your time in loose-fitting athleisure wear.

Not listening properly to a colleague and working to create a solution that's a win for both of you? Hours of emails, arguments, and politics that wastes everyone's time and energy.

Or globally, we have pumped the same amount of carbon dioxide into the atmosphere in the last 30 years as we did in the whole of human history up to 1990? If we carry on in the same irresponsible and thoughtless way, as much as 30–50% of all animal and plant life will be extinct by the middle of this century.

So when Billy turned down that job at a nonprofit because he wanted to make money somewhere where people were driven and commercially minded, he couldn't see the consequences.

Even though George's father had tried to help him.

Which is why George was sitting here now with his old friend . . .

~~~

Billy looked down at his drink. He was remembering one particular evening, what felt like a lifetime ago . . .

"Your father told me to be true to myself. I remember it so clearly now. We were sitting on your garden terrace. It was one of those midsummer evenings, still warm when it was dark. The three of us were sitting outside drinking whisky. I think we were even smoking cigars!"

George laughed. He was back there on the terrace with them.

"I was talking about my career choices. I was saying that I didn't think it was the point of business to do good and that you and I had one choice to make—whether to work for a nonprofit and be happy never making enough money or join a firm where we were free to make as much money for ourselves as possible. I even think I said you were lucky because you could join your Dad's firm and do that."

"Yes. You did."

"And that's when your father told me that the point of his business was to make the world a kinder place. But it didn't make sense to me. You built buildings—shopping malls and offices. Where did kindness fit with that? I still don't understand what he meant."

"Dad believed the purpose of all businesses was to make the world a better place. Not just to make money. He saw it as his duty to use the money he made, the connections and influence he had— basically all the leverage he possessed—to be kind. That's why, for example, we never *just* built shopping malls. We also employed local people and made sure that our planning incorporated community facilities and green spaces. In other words, we were putting something back into those communities. Yes, we were building malls, but we were also leaving a lasting legacy of kindness."

Billy looked at George. Properly, for the first time since they had sat down together.

"What was it you came to tell me?"

George smiled.

This was the moment.

Billy was ready.

"You refused the call.

"And I don't mean all those times you didn't pick up.

"You refused the call of your heart and now you've spent 12 years of your life in work that makes you miserable. Just because you thought what you wanted was money . . . other people's affirmation of your value."

Billy knew what he meant straight away. His mind raced back to that evening when the photographs were taken, Billy, George and the other volunteers sitting around the campfire talking about their ambitions for the future.

Billy wanted to start a water brand. He wanted to "buy one, give one." He wanted people to sit in fancy bars and restaurants with a bottle of water on the table knowing that they were also providing fresh water to people who badly needed it. He knew there was a business in this. He knew that he could make money *and* do some good at the same time. Or, as George's father had said, "You can make money in business and be kind. It's the only sustainable way to do business that I know."

"You had a dream of what you wanted to achieve in business, of how you were going to run your company, of the impact you wanted to make on the world. And you didn't do it."

There was too much history between them, too much truth, for Billy to get upset with George for what he had just said. He was right.

He had refused the call.

Don't refuse the call

"I wish I'd had the courage to live a life true to myself, not the life others expected of me."

This is the most common regret of the dying, as told to Bronnie Ware, a former palliative nurse who is now on a mission to "inspire you to know life without regrets". As she goes on to say:

"When people realize that their life is almost over and look back clearly on it, it is easy to see how many dreams have gone unfulfilled."

Let's remember our numbers. 45 people every minute of every day dying without knowing the joy of work they love.

I hope it is a long time coming, but don't be one of them.

Don't refuse YOUR call.

You believe in the power of kindness.

You believe that when we work with kindness, we thrive and so do the organizations we work in.

You believe that business has the power to do good.

So, how are you called to work with kindness?

Maybe you have a dream like Billy did. Or maybe you simply want to make where you work that little bit kinder.

So do it. Start small but with big ambitions.

Keep at it every day. Do whatever you think it takes to put kindness to work.

But whatever you do, now that you've read this book . . .

Don't refuse the call.

~~~

"I have choices, so I can help you, Billy. It's what my father wanted. But before I can help you, you've got to help yourself."

"What do you mean? I don't understand."

Billy was in a curious state of emotional exhaustion and excitement. He knew George's father back then was trying to steer him to make the choice to follow his dream, to be in business and to be kind. And he knew his old friend was here with him now because he cared, and he had something to say.

"Kindness starts with you, Billy. If you want to start making something of your life, you have to make kind choices for yourself. Nobody else will do it for you. Before you can make a big impact being kind to others, you have to be kind to yourself."

"What, you mean I have to lay off the beer?" Billy joked.

"Well, I like a drink as well, but I make choices that support the impact I want to have on the world. For example, I start every day at 5:30am with yoga, meditation, breathing exercises and journaling. I'm not saying this because I'm boasting or telling you how to live your life. I'm saying it because I've worked out what sustains and nourishes *me*. So I take breaks in the day, get away from the computer, things like that . . . I do whatever feels right so I can be kind to me."

The contrast between them was only too obvious to Billy. Back in the day, he had been the good-looking one and gotten all the interest. Now . . . well, he saw the occasional glances that George was attracting.

"Billy, I know you believe in the power of kindness. Isn't it time you started being kind to yourself?"

Be kind to yourself

If you acknowledge the power of kindness, the natural place to start being kind is with yourself. Kindness isn't something you should wait for. For some other person to be kind and set an example. You're the example. And, most importantly, you're the example to yourself. If you feel good about yourself, it's a lot easier to encourage others to feel the same.

So, find ways to be kind to you.

Because kindness starts with you.

~~~

"If you help yourself, I can help you."

Billy put his drink down and sat forward in his seat. "What do you mean?"

"My father believed that one of the most powerful things you can do with kindness is to pass it on. He was kind to anybody and everybody because he knew that kindness isn't something you 'use up'. In fact, he knew that the more he spread kindness, the more there is in the world. He was especially like that at work. He used to say that, because we spend so much of our lives at work with so many people, it's the perfect place to be kind."

Billy knew the truth of this. There were a few people at work who always seemed to be thinking of others and who were kind. He'd also noticed that, whatever level these people were at, they were also some of the most successful people in the business. They were the ones who were working on the best projects, with the top talent and, if he was honest, at his level doing a lot better than him.

"My father wanted me to help you. And a few other people. So he set up a fund to invest in kind businesses. He wanted you to have the investment to start your bottled water brand."

Billy looked intently at George. He was struggling to process what he has just heard.

"Why me?"

"Because he believed in you and he believed that if he showed that belief in you, you would believe in yourself. Basically, you wouldn't refuse the call, and you'd follow your dream."

"I don't know what to say."

"You don't have to say anything, apart from 'yes' and 'thanks'. This is why I came to find you . . . because I believe in you, even though you wouldn't take MY call!"

Be kind to others

If you allow yourself to think deeply, just for a moment, about the concept of ecosystems and the fact that everything in the physical world is interconnected, you get a glimpse into why kindness is so powerful. Whether you're coming at it from a scientific perspective or from a broader, more spiritual standpoint, this interconnectedness is undeniable.

When we go out into the world expressing anger and hatred, it feels bad—both physically and mentally.

When we go out into the world expressing kindness, it feels good.

In other words, every time that you are kind to a friend, a colleague, a stranger, an animal, or indeed any sentient organism, you are ultimately being kind to yourself.

It's worth remembering that.

So, however you can be. Be kind to others.

You might not be able to invest in somebody's business. But that doesn't matter. Kindness isn't usually about the big impacts—it's about lots of little things that together add up to a big impact.

We are all so deeply interconnected. As I sit here writing this story of kindness, I know it will encourage you to be kind to yourself and to be kind to others.

Why?

Because I believe in you.

~~~

The deed was done. Kind Water had the investment it needed to get started.

"Last orders, ladies and gentlemen, please."

George drained his glass and got up to put on his coat.

"One last thing."

"You are a Kindness at Work Champion. The success of kindness in your business will carry kindness from north to south and east to west in a wave of humanity that literally has the potential to save the world. The planet now and future generations are all relying on you."

"No pressure then," Billy smiled as he downed his drink. He put his arm around his old friend. "Don't worry, we've got kindness on our side. We can achieve anything."

Be kind to the planet

The world needs kindness now more than ever.

Mental health is at an all-time low; depression and anxiety are considered normal.

Communities are increasingly polarized, with simmering tensions between the haves and have-nots.

A global health pandemic has made us realize how vulnerable we all are and that only a collective response can cure us.

More dangerous still, we are slowly destroying our own habitat, choosing self-gratification and quick wins over sustainable solutions that might give our planet half a chance of survival.

As the world's most loved naturalist Sir David Attenborough has said, "The future of humanity and indeed all life on Earth depends on us."

No pressure then.

But I'm not worried.

Because I believe in you.

I believe that kindness has called and that you, like me, and everybody who reads this book, won't refuse the call.

And that, one day, I'll read your story of kindness at work.

Imagine (Do No Harm)

Cole Baker Bagwell

Kindness. We like to receive it. We know it's good. But what is it *really*? Well, Merriam-Webster defines kindness as "the quality or state of being gentle and considerate." That sounds lovely but there's *so much* more.

Every major world religion from Christianity to Islam calls for us to practice kindness in one powerful way or another. Messages about kindness adorn bumper stickers, baseball caps, t-shirts, face masks, sweatshirts, notebooks, and other useful things. It's become a popular message delivered by actors like Brad Pitt, singers like Lady Gaga, and politicians like Joe Biden. We hear stories about the kindness of strangers that spark something deep within us and warm our hearts. We engage in "random acts of kindness," and we "pay it forward" because of the way kindness makes us feel. And an array of neuroscientists, psychologists, and researchers (from some very well-known institutions) have made kindness the focus of their work. They're studying why we have those yummy feelings and the impact kindness has on our minds, bodies, and relationships.

Kindness is *so much* more than "gentle and considerate." So, what if thinking about kindness in a deeper way could help us redefine it? And, *what if* **redefining kindness** and *living into* our new definition could positively transform every one of us and the world as we know it?

I took my first yoga class in 1994. I was in my mid-twenties, and life felt super hard. I was racing through fast food drive-throughs and calling it nourishment. My stress level was off the charts from spending eight hours a day at a job that paid my bills but left me feeling like a cog in the capitalist machine. I was pouring all of my energy into a relationship that was terrorizing my soul and forcing me to abandon the healthy relationships I needed most. I spent the lion's share of my days in a tornado-like loop, shapeshifting to fit into the toxic situations I'd chosen. That was my reality. It changed the morning I noticed the number "11" forming on the skin between my eyebrows. It was gaining prominence from furrowing too often. I knew I needed to find balance and regain something I sensed I'd lost. I couldn't put my finger on exactly what that "something" was, but I could feel that it was gone.

I talked with a friend about how far away I felt from myself. She told me about yoga and the wave of calm she enjoyed after communing with her mat. Calm was a step in the right direction.

I found a studio that day and signed up. On the night of my first class, I hit traffic after work, which caused me to screech in mere minutes before the start time. I darted inside like a Tasmanian devil, breathing heavily and juggling my keys, my purse, and my mat. I was greeted at the door by a woman named "Felicia" who radiated an energy that was steady, knowing, wise, and kind. She met my eyes gently and said, "Welcome." The few seconds of silence that came after that were disorienting. I quickly filled the space by telling her I was new to yoga and that I didn't know a thing. She smiled warmly and said, "Yoga's great, but mindfulness will change your life." Felicia turned out to be right, and to this day, it's one of the most powerful life tools I've learned. If you're wondering what yoga has to do with this book about kindness, hang in there. We're heading that way.

As the days turned into weeks and months, the mindfulness I practiced on my yoga mat became like air for me. It ignited something visceral that I'd forgotten. The more I practiced, the more it flowed into every part of my life. Gradually, I became more aware and connected with myself. I understood my choices that served me well and the ones that caused me to suffer. I stopped judging myself. I woke up earlier, meditated, gave gratitude, and I ate good things from my own kitchen. I left the toxic relationship and the job. I started seeing people and situations through a more objective, forgiving, and hopeful lens. I saw new possibilities because I changed the way I approached everything. My true self started surfacing, and I found balance that allowed me to live kindly.

I needed to understand what I was experiencing and why. So, I started studying everything I could about the history of the ancient practices of yoga and mindfulness. I read about early spiritual seekers and what prompted them to leave everything behind and go into the woods for days to sit silently. I learned they sat because they were seeking enlightenment. They were trying to connect with their truest nature and, ultimately, with something far bigger than themselves. Their instinct guided them to discover their nature long before neuroscientists, researchers, and MRIs were available to teach them. I realized the reason I came to my mat to sit was to connect with my nature and something far bigger too.

The ancient yogis didn't just sit. They created a set of ten rules for themselves—the Yamas and Niyamas—to serve as a foundation for their behavior and choices. I've spent years studying, contemplating, and quietly practicing these rules. The first took up permanent residence in my soul. It's called *Ahimsa*. It's my most favorite, and it brings us right here. (Thanks for sticking around.)

Ahimsa is a Sanskrit word that means "compassion, non-violence." It means **do no harm**. I believe this is **the highest form of kindness** because it provides the foundation that helps us *live into* compassion—a capacity and emotion that neuroscience has proven is innately human. That's right. Every single one of us is born to be compassionate. The struggle I experienced in my twenties came from disconnecting with my true nature. It prevented me from being kind to myself, which made it difficult for me to share and attract kindness. Once I put the pieces of that puzzle together, my life changed.

So back to my initial question of what kindness really is. The way we define, think about, and value kindness sells it short. Some of us get squirrely just saying the word out of fear that it will make us look "soft" or weak. Many of us think it's a thing we do at the holidays or on occasion. In that case, kindness becomes transactional. The truth is **kindness** is a form of strength and a proliferating force for good. We have to think deeper.

Kindness isn't new. In fact, the first mention of the word dates back to the 14th century where it was defined as "noble deeds or courtesy." In my estimation, the greatest noble deed and courtesy we can offer one another is a commitment to **do no harm.**

I've come to realize that kindness isn't a quality at all. Rather, it's a **capacity born of compassion and intention** that marries the heart with the mind. This capacity is derived from our truest nature. It has the power to change the world because it changes the way we show up, connect, build trust, and navigate life together. I know this because I boldly brought kindness into one of the most unlikely places—the business world.

I worked in corporate America for two decades. From Wall Street to Silicon Valley, I saw a steady rise in the numbers of us who are struggling with epidemic levels of anxiety, depression, loneliness, and disconnection. It was heartbreaking. In every case, I considered the root cause. I realized what we're fundamentally suffering from is a lack of kindness. It's impacting every one of us, the choices we make, and the connections we share.

I led my work with a commitment to do no harm—just like the ancient yogis. My commitment to the highest form of kindness guided my thoughts, words, and actions. It was the foundation that allowed me to work with integrity, curiosity, patience, and persistence. It helped me bring people together to accomplish some pretty incredible things. (And, we had fun!) My corporate lessons were transformative. They opened my eyes to the possibilities that exist in one little commitment to kindness. I understand its power, and I believe it's the pivot point that enables us to realize our own greatness.

I left my well-paying career in 2019 to share what I experienced and help people connect the dots to discover their own natural magic. I launched a business dedicated to redefining kindness and putting it into motion as a foundation for life and business. I see possibilities everywhere. Here are a few that cause me to spring out of bed every morning.

Imagine how different life would be if all 7.8 billion of us who inhabit this world made one commitment to kindness—to do no harm in all things.

Imagine how this commitment could change our mindset, the way we treat ourselves and one another. Give some thought to how it could change the choices we make. Now, imagine how our kind choices could change our families and our communities. Imagine how this commitment could impact violence and lead us to solve problems without guns or bombs. Imagine how it could fuel us to take care of strangers and bring us together to serve, to ensure that every person has what they need to thrive.

Imagine how this one commitment could change our habits that create our choices. Imagine how this could change the way we communicate, behave, and respond. Imagine how a commitment to this type of kindness could change our priorities and all the things we hold dear.

Imagine how this commitment to kindness could change the investments we make in energy, money, and time. Imagine how committing to do no harm could positively impact our schools, teachers, and the front line workers who care for us during the hardest parts of life.

Imagine our places of work where 3.3 billion of us spend the majority of our waking hours for ⅓ of our lives. Imagine how this type of kindness could change the way we hire, fire, engage, compensate, create, promote, and work together. Imagine how committing to do no harm could change the decisions we make about manufacturing, materials, labor, and wages. Imagine how this could ensure that policies and agreements protected companies

102

and customers equally. Imagine how this one commitment could ensure transparency and fair treatment for everyone.

Imagine what the extraordinary commitment to kindness holds for our leaders. Think about our country, our discord, and division. Think about the very real human challenges we're facing globally. Imagine how a shared commitment to do no harm could enable us to find the common ground needed to solve conflict. Imagine how this foundation could change the way world leaders make decisions and govern. Imagine how this highest form of kindness could change our legal systems and prisons. Think about 2020, and imagine how this commitment could replace ego with objectivity so we could hear one another, gain understanding, transition power, and form relationships built on mutual respect regardless of our gender, age, skin color, or preferences. Imagine how this commitment to kindness could help us develop the trust we need to meld our minds without needing to control and create solutions that benefit every human being and every living creature on our planet.

Imagine the possibilities we could realize by redefining kindness as a commitment to do no harm and then putting that commitment into motion. This is all possible. We just have to change the way we think about kindness and say "yes" to something bigger than ourselves.

Living Kindly

Share Your Spare

Debbie Lundberg

When you think about kindness, do you think of it as an attitude or an act? Do you believe kindness to be a feeling or a function? Do you sense kindness to be a lifestyle or a life goal? And, is kindness at one's core, or is it a choice?

As you contemplate those four theoretical questions, please consider these three experiential questions as well:

Have you ever seen someone perform in the street or a club/bar, or heard a really good song being played by a live musician outside of a sporting venue and then dropped some money in their cup, tip jar, or an instrument case? Remember how good it felt to let that person know you saw and heard them?

Now, have you ever donated a little bit more formally by participating in a GoFundMe or by making a donation to a national or local organization through Venmo or PayPal or a debit or credit card? Remember how good it felt to know that there would be a lasting impact?

Finally, this one is very personal—hopefully you are reading this book with some privacy as you think about this . . . Have you ever given someone a present that you were given for your birthday,

Christmas, or another occasion? I mean right when you were getting it you thought this is so perfect for so and so. And then, you did it . . . you wrapped it up and regifted it. Sure, there was a little bit of intrigue and excitement because you could have gotten "caught" in the act of the regift, and yet remember how good it felt when that person liked the gift, and you were able to share in that joy of giving together?

Imagine if you could generate goodness and fuel those feelings simply with the use of your body . . .

I don't mean doing anything illicit or illegal!

There is a way to utilize your body for good and for feelings of goodness!

How so?

Sure, there are many ways to live kindly through your body, including donating blood or bone marrow or registering to donate your organs or tissue upon death. Mine is a story of a different type.

Early on a Sunday right before my birthday in November of 2019, I was scrolling through social media prior to golfing and saw a post forwarded from a woman I barely knew from some local events.

What I knew about her at that point was that she was a foodie and a baby boomer, and she was open about her opinions. (In contrast, I'm an athlete with food allergies and a Gen X-er, and I write an etiquette column.) We both love and participate in our community. It was kismet that her "news" popped up in my feed as something shared from a page she created called Debra's Kidney Transplant

Journey. It had been a page for a year, and since it hadn't appeared in my feed, I was unaware this woman was in need of a kidney. The reality is that I don't believe in 2019 I knew the term for kidney failure was "renal failure," but I do now!

Consuming the information, I immediately thought, "How can I assist this woman?" and my internal replies were to encourage her, reach out, and be supportive. Perhaps I could offer complimentary coaching to her. My day was filled with ideas . . . none of which included donating my kidney. My mind settled on the idea that I would see her soon, and since I did not have her phone number or email address, at that gathering, I would quietly pursue a few moments with her to offer support.

Not many days passed, and we were both at a huge event for our local chamber. I thought I would ask her how I could help, but we were both volunteering for different fund-raising efforts. It was not appropriate to holler across a festive venue to ask about her kidney situation. Next time, I thought. Next time . . .

Within weeks, we were seated across from one another at the same table at a chamber event, yet it was a round of 10, so the opportunity was nearly lost. Once a member stood up to share what their business did, I pounced. "Debra, Debra, Debra," I whispered. She finally looked up, and I said "Perhaps that is a place where we can do your Dining with Debra together as Dining with the Debs." She nodded in agreement.

My schedule had me traveling about 60% of the time. I loved it, and still love what I get to do for a living. Thankfully, Debra coordinated schedules, and it took until February 18, 2020, for a lunch date. A funny thing about me is that I rarely have lunch with other people outside of luncheon events during the week. My husband, Michael, and podcast co-host, Barb, tease me that they feel like it is a special holiday if/when we have lunch on a weekday. It is not that I am anti-social, rather because it is such an honor to have businesses and individuals confide in me, that my midday hour is spent regrouping or ensuring I am not carrying forward what I just experienced or coached. Still, I was compelled to learn about Debra's condition.

At the planned time, we sat in a booth, ordered, and chatted about our businesses. Realizing it was getting close to the time for me to leave to be on time for my first afternoon client, I finally asked Debra about that kidney post. She shared that her kidney health had deteriorated to the point of being on the transplant list the prior January. Apparently, according to Debra, I asked her "What would make someone donate a kidney?"

Noticing the time, we took a picture for her Dining with Debra social media, and I excused myself and wished Debra well, thanking her for arranging the lunch. She got my phone number for texting the photo.

That night at home, my husband and I talked about how challenging that looming "need" for a kidney must be for her and her husband. I decided I'd get my blood tested. For some strange reason, I could not recall if my blood type was A+ or B+. I remembered the positive part and could not locate my blood donor card that indicated the type. Going into my medical portals left me unsure as well.

The next day, I was flying to Dallas to speak. The desire to do something specific for this woman was strong. On the Amazon app, I typed "blood type test," and wouldn't you know it, for $9.99, anyone can figure out their blood type. So, I ordered it, spoke in Houston the next day, and flew home that night. Wheeling my carry-on behind me, I kissed my husband, grabbed that familiar box with the smile on it, and went right into the primary bathroom. I pricked my fingers and awaited the results. In the meantime, I thought, "How will I get in touch with Debra?" I scrolled back in my texts to her text with the photo from our lunch. Then, I sent a photo of the dried results with a text to Debra stating, "A+ Will that work?"

Naively, I thought if we were a blood type match, she could have my kidney, right? Not so fast . . .

As shocking as this may seem, the local transplant team at Tampa General Hospital, would not accept an Amazon-delivered blood type test as proof that my kidney would work for Debra, so on February 28, the first blood draw took place.

That Friday, the last Friday of that month, was quite memorable, as when I arrived at the transplant facility less than 5 miles from our home, it was apparent that most people who were there were not like me. Not many people there were without a health heaviness to them or someone with them. The staff was friendly, the facility was bright and clean, and yet there was awareness that these were people seeking kidney and liver transplants.

When I was called back for the blood draw, the positive energy there was palpable. When they all said it was nice to meet me, I felt it. When they said they hoped to see me again soon, I knew they knew if I did come back, it was possible, and even probable, that someone might have their dream of a new kidney come true. I was both excited and overwhelmed briefly. What if I wasn't a match? I dried my tears as I exited the elevator, and a calm came over me. I will be a match.

It wasn't a wish; it was more of a fact.

I called Michael and told him that I felt inexplicably confident I would be the donor. He said, "You aren't usually off on these feelings," and shared that he supported me. Next, I called Debra with the same update. She asked me "Why are you doing this for me?" and as a trainer who encourages clients not to ask "Why" questions because they make people feel defensive, I took a breath and said, "It's less about the why and more about the why not. I do not see a reason not to do this. If I have had two kidneys for 50 years, I can live on one, and you need one. Isn't doing this simply the right thing to do?" We agreed that for both of us, the end of the year would be the best time for the transplant to take place.

Without official test results, I told two physicians of my intentions. Michael and I flew to California to see my aunt and uncle. Even though donation was a recent decision, we decided to tell them. They were surprised, supportive, and had questions. On the golf course that first Friday in March, I received a call about the results only to return the call too late. Still, Michael and I spent one night at dinner researching all the donor requirements, experiences, and life-long impacts of living with one kidney. We golfed, had a ball, and flew back to Florida.

I heard from Tampa General Hospital that our blood was a match and scheduled the urinalysis process.

Then COVID-19 hit.

On Friday, March 13, when we thought the shut-down would be two weeks, I decided to post something encouraging about 10,000 steps a day for positivity. My running partner, Lynn, loved the idea, and the hashtag #KindnessNeedNotBeQuarantined began. One photo was posted daily with an encouraging message. The experience and album were called "10,000 Steps to Sunrise," as I am a 4:31 AM riser, and getting a workout in early means the day is open to all opportunities (and kindness sharing)!

Meanwhile, the donor assessment continued, masked, alone, and feeling committed to this woman seen last at the February lunch. At the suggestion of my doctor, I shifted my workouts to less weights and even some walking in place of running to ensure my hormones and all numbers would be in the best place for the testing. At the same time, my business and travel came to a halt. I had over 30 gigs that were being postponed or cancelled. I had no revenue and nowhere to speak.

Instead of being frustrated and down, positively contributing was most important, so I offered to give clients and community organizations complimentary sessions for them and their employees or volunteers regarding how to work successfully remotely (After all, I'd done that most of my career). I ended up delivering over 50 Zoom, Teams, Skype, and/or WebX sessions, all the while bringing in only $2,000 in new client revenue. That total was missing a couple of zeroes versus what my history and my goals were, yet that was only proof to me that people could really use more kindness and more complimentary coaching. I kept providing it, and even wrote a book called *REMOTE WORK ROCKSTAR* in the process. I mailed over 100 books out to people who I thought would be interested, may not be able to afford to buy one, or both.

An encouraging message in each of them meant someone would likely know they were being thought of that day, and that perhaps that kind word would lift them up. I also started sending out workday videos about remote work, kindness, and perspective. People started messaging me about how much the tips, books, and sessions were positively impacting them. That was payment enough for me!

Around the time that I was writing the book, Lynn noticed my workout changes. Having a week's worth of testing at TGH scheduled, I told her my "secret." She was thrilled to be included. Good thing she is such an open, reliable, kind friend herself, as she ended up signing the legal documents to be Michael's backup to take me to the hospital should I be the donor and to be his backup for caring for me for the six weeks post-donation! Lynn and I decided we would keep up our 10,000 steps a day for 100 days, which would equal 1 million steps under my #KindnessNeedNotBeQuarantined efforts.

With my final test scheduled for June 18, I reached out to Debra to let her know it was planned, and that it seemed like doing the transplant as soon as possible would be best. She reminded me that I agreed to do this at the end of the year, and she still preferred that. While I was hugely disappointed, I reminded myself that the kind things to do, the perspective to keep was that she was likely scared, so I opted to say nothing. I cried after that call, as I really did not want to take myself out of work again at the end of the year. It was on my mind and in my heart that not focusing on that was best. Separately, Candace, my nurse and overall transplant guru, and Lynn were concerned my heartrate might not get high enough for the stress test, and then I'd have to have a chemical test that would take more time to schedule and perform. Lynn and I decided to ready my body for the stress test! How did I "study" for it? We started tracking my heart rate and increasing our speed to get it up. When the highest I got it was 140-ish, I asked Lynn to meet me at our regular 5:00 AM time to run 3.5 miles the morning of my 6:45 AM stress test so I could get tired enough to get my heart rate up for the test.

At the end of the stress test, I asked Dr. A what I ask each doctor or professional I see, and encourage clients to ask in interviews, which is "What is something I have not yet asked you that you think would be good for me to know?"

She smiled and said "I would think you'd like to know what percentile you are in for your age."

To which I said "So, what percentile am I in for my age group, please?"

She held up her index finger, which I interpreted as "one moment while I check."

I said "Okay," and she said "Okay, what?" I said "I'll wait a minute," and she laughed.

"This finger means 'one,' and that 'one' means you are in the top one percentile for your age group."

I was floored by the statement and elevated by the results from my life's work to be in good physical and mental shape.

The testing was done, and now it was time to wait for the board to review everything to determine if I was a good match based on the counselor's, psychologist's, and medical reports. To stay positive and moving forward, I scheduled a December Exchange-o-Rama (EoR), which is typically a quarterly event I host at the house for 20–50 women where everyone brings all their new or gently used health & beauty products, books, clothes, purses, shoes, and home goods to put out for everyone to free shop before we bag up all remaining items to be donated to local charities. 2020 was the 17th year of my EoR events, and in a strange way, what I was doing in the summer was about to be the ultimate personal Exchange-o-Rama! Imagine that what I'd started with three women in the early 2000s was a long experience readying me to voluntarily have a surgeon cut me open and take a perfectly good kidney! Strange, yet excellent preparation, right?

On June 26th, on the 17th fairway, I received a call, *the call*, from Candace letting me know I was going to be a living kidney donor! Michael and I planned to golf that day, as I knew my case was going before the review board. Being in one of my happy places with my favorite person and supporter was the best distraction. I told Michael and called Debra. Boy was I glad we did not have any words over the date, as Candace offered August 5th or 6th, and when Debra was given the choice by me, she said she was good with either, and that was a huge relief. When I got back with Candace, the 5th was taken, so the 6th of August became our date!

Because I felt like it was Debra's news to share, I only told my parents, brother and sister-in-law, a close cousin, and our nephew and his wife prior to her announcing it. When I asked her if, when, and how she planned to share her news, she said she wasn't sure. I offered to write a poem about it. After all, in the 1990s, a friend of mine, Patty, and I had a business called The Gift of Rhyme, where I wrote poems to announce births, engagements, marriages, birthday celebrations, and more. In limerick form, Kidney Cousins was born, and the concept of The Two Debs and hashtag #KidneyCousins, launched.

Almost immediately, requests came in for me to be on podcasts and television shows about my donation. I often asked if Debra could be included so both sides of my #ShareYourSpare story could be heard and that DonateLife.net would get some publicity to grow awareness and registered donors.

Meanwhile, meeting my surgeon was an outstanding experience. He was calm and confident, humorous, expert, and completely available.

Because of the news links on social media, another civilian who had attended the Air War College through the Air Force in 2019 with me heard what I was doing and reached out to tell me he shared his spare with his son. He kindly became my kidney donor mentor. We talked about everything—what to do before surgery, in the hospital, and at home to get back to running. Steve and I are now life-long buddies, and for his insights, he has my gratitude.

As the date drew near, people often said the same thing: "Why are you doing this for someone you don't really know?" "Are you nervous?" and "That is such a selfless act." While my response to the "Why" question is the same as the first time Debra asked it, my other responses were (and still are), "Yes, I was nervous, and yet not frightened," and even though it is charitable to say it is a selfless act, it seems to me to be a self-aware act. I was aware of my situation and another person's situation. Through myself, I knew I could make a difference, so I did.

I texted Debra and asked her to meet me at Tampa General Hospital a half hour before she was scheduled to arrive for surgery. I really wanted to see her and tell her that this kidney she was receiving is now and forever will be hers. It will not be "my kidney" ever again. She agreed, and we were able to get photos, have our husbands meet (they hadn't met except for on Zoom), and have that talk with some hugs.

Even with COVID-19 keeping Michael from coming into the hospital, the anesthesia team was like a party of friends with how thoughtfully they handled the questions and the anesthetization. A friend of a friend who works there popped in to say "hello," too. I felt safe, loved, and in good hands.

Upon waking, I learned Michael was able to secretly reach out to so many of my family, friends, and colleagues in The American Heart Association, The South Tampa Chamber, The Centre Club, MacDill Air Force Base where I volunteer time, and our golf buddies, that the only transplant team member allowed in the hospital brought me over 100 cards, which I read as I came in and out of sleep. My first and lasting question throughout my stay was, "How is Debra and her third kidney?" (Yes, they add the kidney, and do not typically remove the existing kidneys in the recipient.) It was a relief to learn she was receiving her new kidney well, and while I really thought I'd be able to see her before exiting the hospital, that was not in the cards. My husband checked with Debra's husband, Jim, and we kept texting after she was able to engage.

With Steve's good counsel and my surgeon's recommendations followed, I walked the halls in the hospital and stayed only about 36 hours versus the three–four days planned. Even the chef of the hospital spent time sharing with me how to heal through food.

My surgeon said that while he couldn't guarantee it, if I would give the surgery four full days of rest, I'd likely be back to my 10,000 steps a day in segments before I saw him at my two-week post-surgery appointment. He was right: I was. And I attribute that success to his excellent work, my feeling great going into it, and all the support from people I know, from Debra's family, and from complete strangers. The outpouring of appreciation and admiration was humbling and so very kind. Additionally, someone who heard my story invited me to join the Kidney Donor Athletes (KDA) group online, and that group of people who were athletes prior to donation, have been an outstanding network of like-minded people all over the world. While there are only a couple hundred of us (now Steve is in the group, too!), it has been a source of ideas and insights.

With all the publicity prior to the transplant, and all the stories since, it is still tremendously heartwarming to hear from a stranger, acquaintance, or friend a quick "thank you" in a card, text, or call. Knowing that telling my #ShareYourSpare journey gave people hope in a time of strange uncertainty and that others have registered to be donors means this donation, this experience, did not end with Debra and me, and that positivity and kindness can beget more kindness and positivity!

Additionally, Tampa General Hospital's Patient and Family Advisory Council (PFAC) asked me to join their board to positively impact future patient and family engagements. I accepted. And, separately, it was pure joy to deliver a virtual keynote with my surgeon to the 600 members of the surgical team at Tampa General to end a perioperative week celebration. Michael met Dr. Huang, finally, and throughout the brief time together, he was nothing but gracious and generous. To spend an hour 106 days post-donation recounting my story—with specific gratitude for people I met along the way—felt like getting to be a little part of a secret society of heroes who deserve all the kindness they can get!

While this chapter is about to close, this story need not end. I am now known as #OneBeanerGolfer and #OneBeanerRunner and #OneBeanerPerformanceCoach. As a mentor for other potential donors, encourager of all my KDA friends, and someone who lost 150 grams (the weight of a kidney), while gaining so much more appreciation for people's similarities and differences and the incredible abilities of people and our bodies, I am grateful for the experience!

Most importantly, Debra is doing well. I wish her all the best in all she does! That was one regift for which I am glad I got caught giving to my #KidneyCousin!

So, what are the lesser takeaways? Four points come to mind:

Pain & discomfort. The pain was FAR LESS than ever imagined, and the discomfort was far different than anticipated. The pain is gone. I had pain, true pain, at a low level through the 4th day only. It was a 2 out of 5 at most. I am grateful for that, and I'm still working through the discomfort. The tugs on the skin, the overdoing it at times brings that discomfort right back. Other donors say they have some discomfort forever when lifting weights or pushing their limits. The protrusion in my lower abdomen feels strange, admittedly, and yet the four scars are not a big deal to me. Dr. Huang calls it a "Badge of Honor," and still, many people state they won't go through the process due to the scarring. It never crossed my mind that a few marks for life would keep me from contributing to someone else's extended life and quality of life.

Sleep & rest. Never underestimate the need for sleep (no, not "speed," "sleep!"). Prior to donating, I could sleep at the drop of a hat. Before donating my right kidney, I trained myself to sleep on my back (before stomach sleeping was typical for me). Even though that habit was formed, sleep became strange and disrupted. I highly recommend that anyone who has surgery should get a recliner first. A recliner was my resting place, and somewhere to get a lift where needed. We ended up buying a sleep number bed after a week of the crazy battle to get zzzzs, and it seems to be working. I was a huge proponent of 20-minute power naps previously, and I still am now! The tiredness was shocking and still kicks my butt, even though I am working out, eating clean, and walking and/or running 25–35 miles a week.

People & personal. People have been spectacular supporters. The generosity of strangers has been heart-warming. The consistency and kindness have inspired me to do even more! A meal train was established for dinners for three weeks—how incredibly cool and kind. Others have been radio silent, and that works, too. I won't be upset, yet I will be excited to see some people more than others. Going through the four-part change process I refer to as Impact/Recovery/Healing/Excellence, I am in healing and plan to move through and achieve excellence. Every card, text, and message of thoughtfulness that I received in this journey was personally a point for pushing. People say, "Don't take things personally," and yet we are persons, so how else will we take them? The personal touches people gave me were, and are, valued! Michael, my husband, was an exceptional support, and having a team of eight dear friends and confidants communicating out was reassuring, too.

Identify & Identity. As proud as I am to identify as someone who gave a kidney, a #OneBeaner, and to be a living organ donor, a label is not my sole identity. This has changed my life because of habits such as water intake, bathroom planning, and protein lessening. They are aspects of how I function, and not my only function or focus. Please see me as Debbie Lundberg, and all I do, and being a kidney donor as something for which I identify with and offer in hopes of encouraging others. Additionally, I get to be the very humbled and proud wife of a kidney donor, for my husband, Michael Lundberg, chose to donate to a stranger after living through this experience with me and being inspired by it.

Understandably, you may or may not opt to #ShareYourSpare, and that is certainly up to you. Still, know that each time you tip, contribute, and recognize someone's effort, your kindness feels good to you, and lets others have a good chance at feeling good, too!

Now, having read this, you likely have surmised that kindness is, in fact, an attitude AND an action, kindness is a feeling AND a function, and kindness is a lifestyle AND a life goal. So, whether it has always been in or at your core or not, please, please, please CHOOSE KINDNESS!

The Kindness of Listening

Daniel Levin

Sitting to write a chapter in the collaborative book *Living Kindly*, I can't help but feel the mantra-like resonance of those two simple words as they enter me. I am struck both by the enormity of impact that living this way could bring to our world and also by the simplicity of its practice, and in that moment I feel awe pass over me, as effortlessly as the voluminous white cloud moves through the sky. It hits me, and suddenly, I realize anew, the magnitude of what kindness really is.

I look forward to reading the rest of the entries of those who contributed to this blessing of kindness to feel how kindness touches them. A million different ways this kindness is expressed and practiced, all right, none wrong, and another cloud of awe strikes me as I see again and again how beautiful and kind this world truly is.

The irony of all of this is, as I sit here and write these words, we are in the final days of a year that has completely challenged us—2020. We are living in one form or another of isolation due to a global pandemic. A vaccine has been created with incredible speed, and yet over half the country does not trust it. Politically, the country is torn apart. People of color want us to know their lives matter. Women no longer sit quietly allowing men to take advantage of them sexually. Everywhere it seems people want to be treated equally. We have lost trust in our government and our institutions. Our corporations are filled with lies and manipulation. We don't know who to trust or even if the news we are hearing is true anymore.

So how is it possible for me to sit here and say I am in awe of this beautiful and kind world we live in? It wasn't always this way. But things happened that completely changed the way I saw the world, and the world that I saw changed then too. These things altered the way I choose to live my life. Those changes of perspective were the greatest gift of kindness one could ever be given.

Four stories changed me. They redefined my purpose in being here; they rotated the trajectory of my life. It is these four stories that I want to share with you now.

~~~

I always wished my life would be the same as everyone else's; that I would grow up, go to college, and enter my father's business. I always thought how nice it would have been to move into a house a few blocks away from my childhood home and maintain long, heartfelt friendships with people I had known all my life, but my life did not have that blessing.

My parents passed away when I was a boy, and that single event propelled me from the innocence of the world I grew up in, to a world I could have never even imagined existed. A three-hour plane ride, the departure point, the lower middle class life I was born into; the destination of an elite upper class life of world renown that had suddenly opened to me.

That three-hour plane ride opened a door for me to become friends with the sons and daughters of some of the richest people in the world. I didn't meet them in lecture halls listening to them speak, but around their dining room tables. They were kind enough to share with me both the blessing of their life and the pains they have experienced. They were generous enough to give me counsel and even kinder, on occasion, to ask my advice on something they were thinking to do.

Having studied in a seminary on Mt. Zion in Jerusalem, Israel, and then to become a traveling monk based in a monastery in the foothills of the Sierra Nevada Mountains, and then later still, to be the director of business development leading Hay House from $3 million in yearly sales to $100 million in yearly sales, I had the amazing good fortune to be close to the people who inspired millions through their books and their live public appearances, and I have had the pleasure to break bread with them and meet their families.

We spoke about the intimate things people only share in the presence of people with whom they feel safe, and I, to this day, still feel so honored to be amongst the small group of people they trusted. They were kind enough to offer me counsel on things in my life and to ask my counsel on things in their lives too. I learned from them how to hold space for real conversation, a gift I still to this day cherish.

And I have sat on street corners in towns and villages all around the world with some of the poorest of the poor. Many times, I didn't speak their language, but still they managed to introduce me to their friends, and somehow, I understood from them that these were the ones with whom they felt safe, the ones who protected them and had their backs.

The meals we shared and the ambience in the places we ate were far from the elegant environments I shared with the richest of the rich, but the feeling of love was just the same. The food we ate was often a loaf of freshly baked bread, an assortment of cheeses and a bottle of wine that I brought to share with them; the ambience: a dirty and torn cardboard box, on a cold dark street in a neighborhood most would be scared to enter. As we sat together, the differences melted away, and for those few moments we were brothers and sisters sharing a love so deep it was hard to fathom.

With all the people I have met, who would have thought that the most impactful people in my life would be a developmentally delayed girl, fictional characters I made up for my book *The Mosaic*, a homeless man sitting on a street corner in downtown San Diego, and a woman 21 years younger than me who I asked to be my wife? Who would have thought these four incidents would completely uproot my life, change my purpose, and invite me to receive what I now believe is the greatest gift of kindness one could ever be given? Certainly not me.

Story 1: How a Developmentally Delayed Girl Who Didn't Speak Taught Me to Listen

The developmentally delayed girl I speak of is my daughter, Elisa. She is 31 years old, and to this day, I have never had a conversation with her. You see, Elisa can't talk like you and I. When she speaks, people don't understand her. "Yes" and "no," sound so similar that it is hard to distinguish her preference.

But, somehow, I understand her more than most people do. It has become my purpose to hear what she is trying to say. I feel closer to my daughter Elisa than to anyone else in my life, and I want her to know I am listening to her and hearing her as well. Many times, because of how close we are, I have a pretty good sense of what she is trying to say. But there are also times I have no idea what she is saying.

When she speaks and I don't understand her, she will start to yell. If that doesn't work, she will throw a tantrum. That can happen in a restaurant, a store, driving in a car, or over at a friend's house. When she tantrums and I still don't understand her, she will attack me by trying to rip my shirt or bite me. This pattern of behavior went on for almost 15 years, with incidents like this happening sometimes five, or even ten times a day.

 Finally, one day in the midst of her rage, I couldn't take it anymore, and I said to her, "Elisa I can't do this anymore. You know I love you more than anything in this world, and you know I want more than anything to understand what you are saying, but I cannot understand your words. Can you please find a way to tell me what you are saying without using words?"

Her look of rage changed as a smile came over her face, the kind of smile that melts you all the way down to the core of your heart, and she looked me in the eye and said in perfect English, "I am, Daddy."

I was dumbfounded. When I asked her how she was doing that, she pointed to the side of my head, and I understood from her gesture what she was telling me. She had been speaking to me telepathically, putting thoughts into my head. As she said this, I realized, I had heard her thoughts many times, but never trusted my instincts. Suddenly, both of us started laughing contagiously, uncontrollably. We laughed for about 20 minutes straight. That is a long time to laugh without stopping. Try it.

Do you know from that moment four years ago until today, Elisa has never acted out again. Once she felt listened to, she no longer needed to yell, tantrum, or attack to be heard.

If that was the end of the story, it would have been amazing because I love that my daughter and I were so happy we found a way to communicate with each other better. I have always dreamed and still do of having a real conversation with her, but at least now, sometimes I can hear what she is trying to say to me. It is amazing how often we take the simplest things for granted, when the simplest things are the most important things in our lives.

Elisa taught me something that day. I realized that everyone has a voice, and when we find a way to listen to them, our lives become richer and filled with more possibilities.

And so I wondered, was Elisa an exception or were the people I work with just like her? Be they CEOs of companies or employees, leaders in government or the people they govern over, teachers in schools or the students they teach, families and community leaders, does everyone have the same basic need to be listened to and heard? Does everyone do the same thing Elisa does (speak, yell, tantrum, and attack) in one form or another when they don't feel heard?

And I found *everyone* does the same thing. When they speak and do not feel heard, they yell. When they yell and they do not feel listened to, they create a scene. And when that doesn't work, they attack or try to destroy something. They shoot people in a shopping mall or blow up a building, attack someone's reputation or destroy a marriage. When I look at each situation and retrofit it, I realize, just like my daughter, these people don't feel heard.

So now, I want to expand the work I am doing and take this "Speak-Yell-Tantrum-Attack" formula my daughter showed me into the boardrooms of companies, into prison interactions with inmates and guards, into hospitals and the way we listen to what our bodies are telling us, and into elementary schools and colleges to enhance the way we educate, especially those square pegs we have been trying to fit into round holes. I want to work more with the government and the political parties to see if, in creating a culture of listening, we can work together and change the way we govern, do business, and raise our families. Thank you, Elisa!

Listening to someone no one else listens to is the greatest gift of kindness anyone can ever give, and it is something we can all do! You might like it so much, you start listening to your own inner voice too!

Story 2: The Writing of *The Mosaic*

The Mosaic is a fable about a boy who loses his parents two years apart on the same day, and when he asks the adults where his parents are, they tell him they are in a place called Heaven.

So, the protagonist, Mo sets out in search of the place called Heaven, but the people he meets along his journey are not the holy men and women he expects to meet. The people he meets are ordinary people; a Road Worker and a Trashman, a Juiceman and a Blind Woman, a Gardener and a Street Artist.

He wonders why he is meeting these people and what they can tell him of the place called Heaven. But, as he sits with them and listens to each of them tell him their story, he realizes the person he now sees is entirely different than the person he first saw. And when that happens over and over again, he wonders, do I see anything the way it is, or do I see everything just the way I am?

He tried to imagine what would happen if he could slide himself out of the way, and just see the world the way it is. What would he see then? How could he learn to see what he doesn't see? In this moment, he looks to his right and sees a monk unzipping the sky, inviting him into a parallel reality. It was there, in the space between two spaces, that he met the Wise One, and realized the Heaven he was seeking was in this change of perception, where he saw what he had always seen, now differently.

The Mosaic is a beautiful story that will touch your heart and change the way you see the world. I thought it would take me about six weeks to write it, but it took me three years to finish *The Mosaic*.

Before I sat to write, I would often meditate for hours to tune in and feel what it was I was to write. When I sat, I felt great about what I was writing. I would save it of course, only to come back to the computer the next day to find the file had not been saved, or on another occasion the file was corrupted and unreadable. Another time after I had completed most of the book my computer crashed and the only files that could not be rescued were the files of *The Mosaic*.

Finally, I called together the characters that I created in *The Mosaic* in my mind's eye, as if I were having a Zoom call with them, and I asked them one by one, why they were not letting me finish their chapter?

The answer they gave me was amazing. They told me, "What you are writing for us to say is not what we want to say." And I answered, "In all due respect, you are my characters. I have created you, and I should be able to write what I want you to say."

They responded, "Yes you can, but if you do, we will not let you complete your book. We have been telling you what we want to say, but you have not been listening. If you write what we are telling you to say, your book will be done in six weeks."

I did, and it was. And yet, I still marvel at what happened. Their voices permeated *The Mosaic*, and they were softer and sweeter than mine. What they told me was that this book was being written first for me and then for others. It was important that I receive what was being given to me. You see, I had been writing a book for others. They were writing the book I most needed to read, and they wanted me to include myself in its learning. Once that happened, they told me, many will benefit from this book as well.

So, if fictional characters I made up could speak to me, what it everything in the world could speak to me too? If I would only listen, what would I hear? All too often I did not hear the world speaking to me. I thought to myself, *Isn't it time I start listening?*

Listening is the greatest gift of kindness anyone can ever give, and it is something we can all do!

Story 3: Why Do You Love Me

I was at one of the lowest points in my life. My manufacturer told me three days before we were to ship close to a million dollars of clothing, that he had lied to me and that he had not made a single garment for the order.

I had spent $300,000 to get everything needed to make the clothes for the pending orders. The good thing was, the money we would make when we shipped the clothes would not only cover our costs but make us a nice profit as well. The problem was that he didn't make anything, so there was nothing to sell. And I was now $300,000 in debt.

As a result, I found myself in a state of high anxiety. I had never been in debt before. I always had whatever money I needed to do the things I had to do. Suddenly all that changed. Now, I was dodging calls from credit card companies calling to collect money I didn't have and with each payment I missed they raised the interest rates on the money I owed. My anxiety kept me up most nights worrying about how I could resolve this seemingly unresolvable problem.

The new emotions caused a spike in my blood pressure, and out of nowhere, a guy who had meditated 30 years and had low blood pressure all his life was now taking blood pressure medication to bring his blood pressure down. And there were other complications too. Though the doctors said there was no way the blood pressure medication could cause a level 8 pain to spread throughout my body, the moment I started taking the pills, the pain appeared.

Into all of this strolled Ana, a beautiful Argentine woman 21 years my junior. We met while we were both studying to be coaches in a Tony Robbins coaching program. They had a private Facebook page for people to be able to communicate with each other. In a post on that Facebook page I saw a note from Ana asking if anyone could help her find her passion again. I wrote that I would be happy to have a conversation with her, and we arranged to talk on Skype.

Something happened in that conversation, Ana was filled with an energy she had never before experienced, and she knew from that call, from that moment, that I was the one she would marry.

There was only one problem. She was already unhappily married to a verbally abusive man who would probably never let her go, and I had no desire to be with someone 21 years younger. But you may have heard the old Yiddish saying, "Man plans, and God laughs." Well I am quite sure God was having a big full belly laugh over our situation.

The more we talked, the more Ana realized her feelings were right. Two and a half months after Ana told me she filed for a divorce, her divorce was finalized. It took only two and a half months, which was unheard of, and three days later, I was on a plane flying to Texas to see a woman who told me she loved me without ever meeting me and someone I was falling in love with, for the first time.

I wanted to be sure she knew what she was walking into. I wanted her to know I had no money, no worse than that, I owed over $300,000 in debt and had no way to pay it back. I wanted her to see the size of my tummy. And I wanted her to see how much older I was than she.

I remember standing there in front of Ana during our first face to face conversation and asking her, "Why do you love me?"

Her response changed my life. She answered, "No one has ever asked me why I love them. I don't need a reason to love you. I love you because every cell in my body loves you."

Years later someone asked me, "How can you tell me you love me. You have no reason to love me." To which, I answered, "If people can hate for no reason, why then can't people love for no reason. I do not need a reason to love you, I love you because love is all I know how to do." It was only later that I realized the seed of this feeling had been planted in me by my wife Ana years before. Feeling loved like that—for no reason—made me feel invincible. This is the greatest gift of kindness I can ever give, and it is something all of us can do!

Story 4: A Homeless Man in Downtown San Diego

As I mentioned earlier, I have had the opportunity to be with some of the richest people in the world, but I have also had the amazing opportunity to sit with the poorest of the poor on street corners and meet their families and have those same conversations.

One of those conversations that touched me the most was with Cory, a homeless man I met in downtown San Diego. When I first approached him, he wanted nothing to do with me. He told me, "This is all I have in the world, this is my street corner, please go, and sit somewhere else.

I promise Cory I would not take much of his time but that I just felt the need to be with him for a little while. He told me that every minute he is talking is a moment away from him working, and he needs to make a certain amount a day to help other homeless people who weren't doing so well. I told him I understood and asked him, "How much do you make in a half hour?"

Without skipping a beat, he told me, "I make $5.00 every half hour, $10 an hour, and I cannot afford to lose that." I pulled out my wallet and looked into it and saw I had a $50 bill. So I took it out and handed it to Cory and said, "Hopefully this will cover a half hour of your time."

Cory looked me for the first time in the eye and said to me, "You're strange. Ok, you can sit with me. What is it that you want to know so badly?"

I looked at him and asked, "Cory, you sit here and watch thousands of people walk by all day long, if you could stop them and talk to all of them, what is it you would want to say to them?"

He didn't even have to think about it for a moment, he knew his answer. "I would invite people to find someone they don't know and ask them how they are doing and then spend 10 minutes listening, really listening to their answer."

I asked him, "Of all the things you could ask for, why would you ask that?" His answer told me.

He said, "Danny, I hate being a homeless person. I am ashamed and embarrassed that this is what my life has become. And if that is not bad enough, every day as people walk by, they spit on me, punch me, kick me, and curse at me. I've gotten hardened to that.

"But one day three months ago, a group of young boys came up to me and started punching me and kicking me and beating me. I thought I was going to die. Every part of my body ached in pain, and on top of that, they stole the money I had in my hat too.

"I lay down and asked myself, 'What am I doing here? It seems I am only making things worse. I hate my life, and people seem really mad at me too.' And in that moment as I was lying there with my eyes closed, trying to recover, a man came up and started urinating on me. I was so disgusted with my life that I decided then and there that, when evening came, I would go around the corner to the street behind this street, a dark street no one goes to, and that evening, I would take my life, thinking no one would even miss me.

"Two minutes after I had that thought, a man came out of nowhere, dressed in a three-piece suit. He put his hand on my shoulder and asked me, 'Brother, how are you doing?' Tears started to pour from my eyes, and I told him I wasn't doing well and I asked him to just keep going. But he did not just keep going. He sat down next to me and said, 'I am here for you if you want someone to listen.'

"Danny, I cried and cried on his shoulder and told him all of how I hated my life and how much shame and disappointment I felt and how hard everything had become, and he just listened to me and held me. He didn't try to fix me or help me or change me. He just listened.

"Do you know, it took only about 10 minutes, and when he left, I realized I could no longer kill myself, because a man in a three-piece suit cared enough about me to listen to me for 10 minutes? That man has no idea that he saved my life that day."

Here is another interesting result of this story. It is called The Butterfly Effect, where one small action, like the flapping of a butterfly's wings gets multiplied by others doing the same and over time the flapping of their wings creates a hurricane in another part of the world. Just like that man had no idea he saved Cory's life, Cory has no idea the impact his story had on me. He doesn't know I tell his story and offer his challenge on every TV, radio, or podcast show I am interviewed on and how much that one story touches others. And I offer that same challenge to you today, I ask you to join the millions of people that are now doing this:

Take ten minutes out of the course of your life, go up to a stranger, and just ask them how they are doing. You don't need to help them, fix them, coach them, or convert them. All you need to do is listen.

I am creating a Revolution of Listening. There is no membership fee. There is no church you have to join. All that is asked of you is to care about someone enough to just go up to them and ask them how they are doing, and then listen.

What I have found is no matter how much money you have or do not have, what color your skin or what border you live behind, what religion you practice or don't practice, whether you live in a mansion or a cardboard box, we all want the same three things.

- To be loved and accepted
- To be listened to and heard
- To be acknowledged and validated

And that is something all of us can do for each other. You do not need a degree in psychology or to be ordained a rabbi, minister, or priest to do it. All you need is a heart that truly cares for the wellbeing of others.

We have no idea the impact listening has. I want to challenge each of you to take this challenge and join the revolution of listening. Loving and accepting another person, listening to them and hearing them and acknowledging them for being who they are, is the greatest gift of kindness anyone can ever give and it is something we can all do!

The Intersection of the Four Stories

When I sat with the fact that everyone in the world wanted the same three things from life—to be loved and accepted, listened to and heard, and acknowledged and validated for what they believe—I realized I could give these three things to everyone I met. Gone were the days where I was asked to teach, fix, change, and help, all I was being asked to do now was to hold the space for them to feel safe enough to let down the walls they use to protect themselves and invite them to discover who they are behind those walls. When those walls open up, miracles happen.

And what is the secret that allows people to let down their walls? Kindness. I saw this over and over again in my own life. When I hit myself or put myself down, it hurt, so eventually I built walls to protect me from getting hit. Then Trust. The moment I stopped hitting myself, I realized the only reason now for the walls was that I didn't trust that I would continue to be kind to myself. And then I saw if I listen to myself, I will not need to yell, tantrum, and attack, and those walls could come down.

I learned then and there that the secret to bringing down the walls that keep us from each other is kindness, trust, and listening. So, imagine what would happen if we would all:

- Love others for no reason
- Live kindly
- Listen to each other

Who knows? By doing these three simple things, we might give the world the greatest gift of kindness we could ever give. I invite you to join me. Love for no reason. Live Kindly. And Listen to each other.

Living Kindly

A Kind Journey

Krystle Mabery

On a beautiful spring morning in Florida, around May 2019, I was sitting at my kitchen table watching the sunrise through the window as I started on my second cup of coffee. Back then, two or three cups of coffee each day seemed normal, and sometimes even necessary.

While looking over my to-do list for a project I was managing, I couldn't shake that listless feeling that seemed to overshadow my recent days. Usually when these kinds of thoughts arose, I would remind myself of how fortunate I was to have a great role within a corporate headquarters located less than two miles away from my home. I would remind myself that I'd moved from Virginia just five years prior and had personally accomplished so much; I developed confidence and broke through the dreaded impostor syndrome; I built relationships with many successful leaders who became mentors; I traveled outside of the United States for the first time; I was making a dent in my student loan payments; and through counseling, I finally understood why, despite all I had to be grateful for, I was still so unhappy. Under normal circumstances, this reality check was enough, but for some reason this day seemed different. I couldn't help but wonder, "Do I have it all . . . or does it all have me?"

As I sat alone at my computer that spring day, rigorously working through project details, all of a sudden, dizziness came over me. My chest felt tight, my stomach was in knots, I began to hyperventilate, I felt warmer than the Florida pavement, and I was terrified (which made things worse). There I sat at the peak of my accomplishments, desperately trying to understand what the hell was going on with me. What could it possibly be? At work, whenever someone needed help, I was there. Anytime someone called, I answered. Any day of the week I received an email, I usually responded. Anytime I should have taken a personal day for, let's say, a dentist appointment or checkup, I rescheduled. Any slack that was left on my projects, I picked up. I had been doing this for years. "Duh, it's called 'kindness,' people!" And then it hit me. That wasn't kindness; it was consistently prioritizing everyone over myself. And THAT was my problem!

I later learned that what I experienced that day was a panic attack. I also found that many others have experienced panic attacks in their own lives, and they were almost considered to be common. For me, this was a wakeup call—a big one. My "kindness" had become a liability. Doing for others was what I enjoyed, but doing for myself had always felt like a sacrifice. After months of ignoring the warning signs (insomnia, lack of appetite, acne, low energy, irritability, and an all-consuming hazy feeling of passively "existing" in the world), my body finally had enough. I was officially burnt out from not only being stressed and overwhelmed (which in truth was largely self-imposed), but also from not making myself a priority. After some reflection, I decided that I had to change the direction of my life. But change my life to what, though? I never thought about pursuing a career based on what I really wanted. I typically sought out a job based on the necessity of my circumstances. "So," I thought, "Who am I? And what does this have to do with a career anyway?"

Being kind to yourself gives you the fuel to be kind to others.

Would you say that acts of kindness require an external invitation? Think back on when you volunteered time, gave resources, or donated money. Did they usually originate from a request? I, like many others, viewed invitations as the door to kindness . . . until recently. Recently, I discovered something about kindness that seems so obvious now that I think about it. Without intending to, on my journey to step into my purpose and pivot into a new career, I realized kindness is not limited to behavior alone—it is also a mindset. Kindness can be defined as "the quality of being friendly, generous, and considerate." This mindset was easy for me to adopt toward others, allowing me to recognize opportunities (that I may not have seen otherwise) to positively impact the lives of those around me. But what about applying a mindset of kindness to myself?

It sounds like a rhetorical question, but I believe many people are just like I was . . . friendly, generous, and considerate to everyone but themselves. Self-care, or being kind to yourself, is truly the foundation you need to live and sustain a balanced life. Being kind to yourself also does not require an invitation, and is something that should be done proactively. It took me years to realize how important and fundamental this other aspect of kindness is, but I now know this with certainty—if you do not choose to prioritize yourself, it's only a matter of time before life "invites" you to reconsider.

For years I had not been kind to myself and would like to say that I was unaware, but that would be untrue. The signs were there; I just stubbornly preferred to stick with my perspective on kindness. I was convinced my approach to life was working, until one day it all came crashing down.

Weeks after my panic attack and taking countless personality-career assessments, I was convinced that finding a career that blended my human services passion with my business experience was impossible. Not only that, but I also was unable to imagine my income going from successful to zero! Then one weekend I came across a TEDx video titled, "F* The Fear, It's Not Real Anyway!" Curious and intrigued, I pressed play, thinking, *Is he talking to me?*

It turns out Deri Llewellyn-Davies had climbed and was on Mount Everest during the devastating 2015 earthquake. I won't spoil the rest of his story, but what I will tell you is what his story did for me. The very next Monday, "I woke-up decided." Shortly after I went to work, I walked into my manager's office and gave my notice. Then, I darted upstairs to share the news with a trusted mentor, beaming with a huge smile on my face.

"Great! Which company are you going to?" they asked.

I responded, "Oh I haven't figured that out yet, but I watched this TEDx over the weekend about a guy who climbed Mount Everest, so I figured if he can climb the mountain, I could figure this out." The look of shock and disbelief on their face still makes me laugh to this day. I might as well have told them I was planning to climb the actual mountain itself!

As a general rule, it is ideal to secure a job or at the very least have a solid plan before you step away. I agree 100% with this. It is also best to have savings set aside to support you throughout your transition. I had the savings, and with that, I was ready to embark on my own adventure.

Not long after taking that leap of faith, I came across an announcement for an upcoming retreat on the French Riviera. Dr. Andrea Pennington, another TEDx speaker I followed, was launching a year-long mastermind program which kicked off with a week-long seminar in Nice, France. The workshops would cover the spectrum of business from "branding and your core message, to mindset and focus, to marketing and selling your services in a soul-led way."

Seeing this, I knew it was the guidance I needed, so I booked it. Nearly packed and cautiously optimistic about my first international solo trip, it was concerning to me that I felt more comfortable being myself when I was away from home. I decided that I was going to be confident in who I am and break through my fears—starting now!

So, prior to my departure, I joined local organizations and began attending networking events. To my surprise, my assumptions were wrong! As I entered into these environments with no expectations, just being genuinely curious and open—people were drawn to me. I also discovered the vast possibilities when it comes to turning your passion into a purposeful career. Often, the only real limitation is our mind. I met so many amazing women who love what they do and who they serve. With this refreshing revelation and shift in perspective, off I went to France!

At the seminar, I was blown away by what I saw. I was in a conference room surrounded by dozens of people who were dedicating their lives to helping others locally, nationally, and internationally. Many had built successful careers around causes that were personally significant to them. Most were doing this full-time and were excited, fulfilled, and earning a sustainable income from these careers. Coming from a background in business, it was inspiring and uplifting to see firsthand that I, too, could make kindness the focal point of my career.

Now thoroughly satisfied with my decision to attend this seminar, I thought, "Great, this is what I came here to realize." Then a tall Welsh man rushed into the conference room, hurried because of his tight travel schedule, and began presenting.

As I was patiently sitting there in the front of the conference room, ready for some of that delicious, fresh squeezed fruit juice that came with lunch, something unbelievable happened! The speaker said something about fear. Then, he went on to say something about loving the thrill of adventure. Then, he shared an excerpt from his TEDx presentation about climbing Mount Everest. Could it be? Yes, Deri Llewellyn-Davies was standing right there in the room.

Confirmation or coincidence? Depends on who you ask, right? Sometimes we have serendipitous encounters in life. Either way, when I returned to Florida, I was refreshed and excited about life's possibilities. Determined to focus more on what can be versus what is, I was ready to dive into my next opportunity.

Kindness begins exactly where we are.

After my return from France, the next opportunity to be kind was unexpected. I sought out an opportunity to become a substitute teacher, and after training, I spent the next few weeks subbing at various middle schools across the county. I was initially looking forward to the winter break, but as it approached, something felt different. I was newly single and, being from up north, the holiday season in Florida was hard to embrace without family nearby and the anticipation of a white Christmas. I had adjusted to my new normal, but this year getting myself into the holiday spirit was a struggle. My choices were simple. I could focus inward, honing in on the feeling of depression, allowing my negative thoughts to multiply, or I could focus on the possibilities to intentionally increase my feelings of joy. I chose joy.

Around this time, I received an invitation to join some local festivities, but by then I was already settled on my decision. I decided this would be the Christmas that I was going to be kind to myself and do things that I enjoy, one of which is cooking! I was all in, just as much as I would have been for anyone else.

I set up my tree, decorated, and even went as far as to design a menu for myself. I even spent some time researching recipes and made a lengthy grocery list. Despite the rainy weather, the next morning I arrived at the grocery store by 7:00 AM, recorded a video for my family, and completed my shopping list. When I got home and read their responses, I couldn't understand why everyone was concerned that I was making too much food. On Christmas Eve and by Christmas Day, I had prepared two Cornish hens, four turkey wings, sweet potato casserole, corn pudding, deviled eggs, baked macaroni and cheese, green bean casserole, and a banana pudding. Delighted and exhausted, I then realized they were right, but it was already too late. So, what was I going to do about it?

The next day, I reached out to an acquaintance for help. I knew Leigh Clark had founded a nonprofit organization with a focus on kindness. I also knew her organization especially did many thoughtful things during the holiday season. Over lunch I explained my dilemma and asked Leigh if she knew of anyone who could benefit from the bountiful leftovers. She did!

Within the hour Leigh got me the contact information of a woman who had been living in a shelter with her two children. When I contacted this woman, she was overjoyed by the idea of having a home-cooked meal for the holidays. She explained that there were also other families there who would all be greatly appreciative of anything that I brought.

I spent the afternoon packing up leftovers and looking around my apartment for jewelry, games, and anything that young ones or families might enjoy. On my way to meet her, I swung by the grocery store to pick up some drinks and fresh fried chicken, and then I headed over with my care package. After meeting her and talking for a while, I was in awe of her resilience and determination to not be defined by the setbacks in her life. Then, to my amazement, she explained that she had already thought of ways to pay it forward. She was planning to separate some of the toys and jewelry to share with another shelter. Who would have thought that an act of kindness initially directed toward myself would have such a ripple effect? In the end, I was grateful for how everything turned out and I wouldn't change a thing.

Seize the moment . . . you never know how your kindness will impact others.

Weeks into the new year, I received a phone call with an offer for me to accept a long-term substitute teacher assignment for an eighth-grade class. The permanent teacher had retired over the holiday break and the school was looking for a reliable person to temporarily fill in. I gladly accepted. When I first arrived, my class, along with a few others, was attending a high school prep assembly. I quietly joined the group in the auditorium, sitting off to the side in one of the empty rows. Toward the end of the presentation, the speaker asked the students to pair up for an exercise where they would ask each other questions about their future. I noticed one student sitting alone who didn't have a partner, so I went over to him, and we did the assignment together. At the time I did not know he was a student in my class, and as far as I knew, he was a bright young man who had a promising future.

My assigned classes were split into three levels: Cambridge, Advanced, and Regular. Within days of my assignment, I recognized what I believed to be flaws in this system. Now, I do recall when I was in high school, they offered a similar hierarchy for certain classes. In fact, I was proud to take a few advanced classes. However, this wasn't my concern. My concern was that, based on this hierarchy that was communicated to both teachers and students, there was a polarizing difference in the expectations and perspectives on both sides. Classes where the teacher expected less, the students gave less. Classes where the teacher expected more, the students gave more. I recently came across a TEDx by Quentin Allums that perfectly illustrates the power of this narrative.

In his talk "Why People Should Be Strange on Purpose," Allums describes a brilliant experiment conducted by Harvard psychologist Robert Rosenthal that examined the role of self-fulfilling prophecies and the effects of a teachers' expectations on students' academic performance. At the time, I didn't recognize this as the situation I was in, but I did recognize it was a situation that I should address.

What was also surprising to me was an overview I received about the Regular classes. I was told that the Regular students did not care about learning. I was also told, the Regular students were not expected to learn the material because they were already so far behind. To me, this meant I was to provide the classwork with no real expectation that these particular students would excel or succeed. And it broke my heart when I realized all of the students were aware of this stigma, especially the students in the Regular classes. Not yet knowing how I could help, just that I should, one day I walked into an uninhibited lunch conversation that propelled me into action.

Last to the table, I sat down working to fill the gaps in a seemingly riveting discussion amongst the teachers. For one student in particular, the teachers had given up on him. He was considered to be disruptive, not caring about school or authority. Now, this in itself is probably typical to expect to hear amongst teachers, but it was the story that followed that gave me pause. I soon realized that the student they were referring to was also one of my students and that this student was actually in one of my Regular classes. Not only this, but the student they were referring to was the same student I met in the auditorium on my first day. I hadn't experienced a negative encounter with him before or after I was his teacher, and I had no doubt he had greater potential than his reputation.

One of the teachers shared a situation where this particular student had just returned to class from suspension and was smirking at this teacher from his seat. The teacher stopped teaching to confront the student in front of the class for smirking. As you might have guessed, words were exchanged, and the student was kicked out of class and sent to in-school suspension. When the teacher added that this student was already behind in work from skipping class (and the subsequent suspensions as consequence), I couldn't help but challenge the perspective. Inserting myself into the conversation I asked sarcastically, "So, the solution to the student missing class is to make him miss more class?"

Before I move on, I want to acknowledge that teenagers will be teenagers, so disruption and pushing boundaries is very common. And yes, we all get weary—even in well-doing and even as teachers. However, I couldn't overlook the power of these narratives. It wasn't just a simple difference in the difficulty of the curriculum that I was witnessing. What I was witnessing was a difference in expectation, patience, and opportunity. When I returned to class, I decided to respond with encouragement to every student I interacted with. One student, after I told him that he was smart, replied that no teacher had ever said that to him before. And yep, you guessed it, he was also in one of my Regular classes. That day became Day One of my crusade to ensure that all of my students felt valued and that no student was written off. From that point forward, I viewed each day as an opportunity to build a culture of kindness and respect.

A couple weeks later, something astonishing happened. A shift. The classes where the students were originally unengaged became the classes where I saw the most improvement. The students who were originally either extremely withdrawn or extremely disruptive became some of the students who emerged as leaders. The students who were embarrassed to read became the students who volunteered to read first. The students who habitually talked down about themselves began to believe that they were smart. I was amazed by their transformation!

I didn't accept the assignment with a plan to do such acts of kindness, but I looked at the situation I was in as an opportunity to be kind. By taking pride in how I showed up for those kids, I believe I positively impacted their lives by showing them that change starts within.

Kindness in presence

After the pandemic closed schools in March of 2020, my side hustle became my main hustle. At the time, I didn't realize that my newfound free time would soon open another door to an opportunity for me to be kind. Just as I was starting to find a good work-life balance as a freelance business consultant, I received a phone call. Someone dear to me had called with the heartbreaking news that their pregnancy had become extremely risky and would require them to be hospitalized for constant monitoring. After expressing to me how hopeless they were in figuring out what to do next and how to make it through this without anyone nearby for support, I prayed; then I prepared. Within a week I made arrangements to pack up my work, clothes, and of course my air fryer, and headed out of town. That's when I realized that balance is truly a fluid concept. A balanced life requires constant recalibrating and reprioritizing depending on what is most urgent in your life.

I was soon on my way with my car packed to the brim. My intention was simple: I was going there to provide moral support. A few days after I arrived, their situation turned a terrifying corner. After several complications they were forced to deliver their son three months early.

Overwhelmed with a range of emotions, we were all grateful I was there in person to support them through this difficult time. Over the next couple days, they navigated through countless physicians, appointments, and documents preparing them for the nuances of NICU parenting during the pandemic. Ignoring the feeling of helplessness that tried to overtake me, I began focusing on other necessities and things that were within my control. Sooner than anticipated, they were preparing to return home. I stealthily coordinated with their loved ones to prepare an appropriate welcome that was also considerate of their delicate situation. I was filled with relief and excitement when they returned home amazed by this simple but kind gesture.

As their situation continued to evolve and we were now sharing close quarters, I expected they would sit me down and politely ask me to go home. To my surprise, they did sit me down, not to ask me to leave, but to ask me to stay a bit longer. For someone seeking their purpose, often if you follow a path of kindness, your purpose will become clear. In this situation, I naturally stepped into problem solving mode. I was coordinating with those concerned; I was looking for opportunities to bring joy; I was tracking packages; I was cooking meals; I was anticipating needs; I was simply being myself—friendly, generous, and considerate. At first, I thought that the value I brought to them was in my tangible actions. Though these actions were helpful and appreciated, it was the intangible—

my kindness and positive energy—that they needed most in that moment.

Many times, what people really need is for us to be present. To show up for them (even if not physically) so they have comfort and peace in knowing that even when everything else is uncertain, they can depend on you. Now realizing that my purpose was hidden in my actions all along, I finally understood the value in simply being me and returned home better than I left.

After a few months it was holiday season again and I headed north to spend a week visiting family. It had been almost two years since my last visit. When I made it to see my grandparents, ages 82 and 84, within hours I observed the need for me to make myself available. I believed a reset would benefit everyone, so my week-long trip officially became a month-long trip.

There I was with one carry-on bag worth of belongings, fueled by a determination to allow the caregivers to enjoy their families over the holidays and the will to be present for my family. So, I made a new plan. I knew my grandparents needed their routine, but I also knew I had a little leeway to slip in some variety. The first part of my plan, besides essential care, was to find things they could enjoy. The second part of my plan was to remember to make myself a priority. When you love showing up for others, it's very easy to overcommit at the expense of your health, time, and energy. In this situation, self-care was simply taking time to rest or doing things that I enjoyed. Each day, I tried to do something that would put a smile on their faces, and my own. I'm not perfect, so on days I didn't get it right I would focus on doing better the next day! I hadn't considered, or intended, the ripple effect my initial act of kindness would have.

Just when I thought the days were going according to plan, what I didn't anticipate were the additional opportunities that emerged. While being present for my grandparents, I was also able to spend a few days helping my cousin pack up her house to move, volunteer at a local church for their annual toy drive for underprivileged children, add a nearby family member to my grocery shopping routine who was unable to go shopping for themselves, have lunch with a family member I hadn't seen in years, and even convince my grandmother to ride out with a group of us one evening to see a Christmas light show. She absolutely loved it! Due to my presence and through these acts, my family was also able to have peace of mind, which is truly invaluable. This in itself was a gift, making it a memorable holiday for everyone.

The power of being kind to yourself, being present, and the ripple effect on others

People say that life tends to make sense backward. I can only imagine how my life would have been had I never taken that leap of faith the day I walked away from my job. In retrospect, the fact that my circumstances were not ideal is actually what led me on this purposeful path. The root of philanthropy is "goodwill to fellow members of the human race." To me, this allows for those of us in the initial stages of giving to find creative ways to give back. If we can't spare money, we can give time. If we can't spare time, we can give resources. How we express goodwill will vary. The important thing is to recognize the possibilities in our lives to be kind—now! If we wait for circumstances to be perfect, we may never start.

Over the past few years, three lessons resonated with me the most. First, being kind to ourselves gives us the fuel to be kind to others.

I've lived, and I've learned that making myself a priority is the foundation of a healthy life. When we are kind to both ourselves and others, it allows for a beautiful, sustainable exchange.

Secondly, I learned that kindness begins exactly where we are. Don't discount actions you can take today that may seem too simple or too small. Something that may be small on a grand, global scale still can have a major impact on individual lives, and in the end, that's what makes up the world.

Finally, I learned the power of presence. There is richness in creating a space for people to thrive, and it's almost always reciprocated in some way. When we recognize these moments, we should seize them. Seize the moment to share what you love with others; seize the moment to be compassionate and encouraging; seize the moment to show up for others.

My journey is far from over, which allows me to experience each day as if something great is going to happen! I look forward to seeing how my life, and the lives of those around me, will continue to unfold.

If not Kindness, What are We Influencing?

Mark Shapiro

On November 13th, 2019, I found myself with the amazing opportunity of being a guest on the CBS News 8 morning show in San Diego to highlight World Kindness Day. I was so excited for the opportunity to talk about kindness and to share my story. However, I also figured I'd be asked the dreaded question, "How can we celebrate World Kindness Day with random acts of kindness in our community?"

While "yes," things like pay it forward lines (or what my friend, Houston Kraft calls "confetti kindness") are really sweet gestures, what drives me crazy is that random kind acts are the default starting point when our society addresses the topic of kindness. The reality, however, is that living kindly is a day-to-day practice and isn't always the easy, timely, or obvious choice—despite being extremely important to our collective well-being (not to mention our physical, mental, and social health).

Back to the TV interview . . . even the thought of the morning show host focusing in on random acts of kindness and framing kindness to the public in a gimmicky, highly produced way frustrated me. And sure enough, her first question was, "How can we celebrate World Kindness Day with random acts of kindness in our community?"

In the kindest and most respectful way I could, I pushed back and dove into the misconceptions of kindness, the benefits of kindness, and the infinite possibilities of not being kind just randomly, but consistently.

Equally annoying, this wasn't the 1st time I've been frustrated with the way our world often looks at kindness. When I started my consulting business, KindBiz, and reached out to companies to share about my relationship building and kind leadership trainings, I'd often be met with, "Your work sounds really 'nice,' and we like what you are doing, but I don't think I'll able to sell your training and workshop to upper management."

We are taught the importance of kindness throughout childhood— as an essential trait and relationship building skill—but apparently, our culture questions the role of the Golden Rule in business. While business is powered by relationships, communication, and teamwork, our society and pop-culture glamorizes a cutthroat approach. From iconic films like *Glengarry Glen Ross* to *The Apprentice* ("you're fired") and the on-going notion that "nice guys finish last," we've been subtly (or not so subtly) disillusioned to the idea that kindness can take a backseat in business.

If you are reading this book, I bet you'd disagree that kindness is optional, and given the state of the world and the effects of the COVID-19 pandemic, we have started to see an immediate change in this narrative, as kindness is vital for any business to not only thrive, but survive right now. Needless to say, those same companies who didn't return my calls are now bringing me in to facilitate not one, but multiple kind leadership and relationship building trainings.

But if I'm going to be super real with you, I also had my own misconceptions about kindness.

For the first 30 years of my life, I mistakenly thought that being "kind" was the same thing as being "nice." Wow, was I wrong! Growing up in Minneapolis, Minn., I definitely could be described as "Minnesota nice"—a cultural stereotype seen in movies like *Fargo* where the characters are overly pleasant and agreeable to the extent where it's automatic and a bit phony.

While I always strived to treat others politely and have pleasant interactions, I didn't realize that my commitment to being nice was not only inauthentic at times, but that others could sense it and found it off-putting. In other words, I learned that being nice can actually be the antithesis of being kind and can have the opposite effect.

The difference between "nice" and "kind"

- Being "nice" is an externally motivated disposition to be pleasant, agreeable, and conflict avoidant.
- Being "kind" is an action-driven internal motivation to be caring, helpful, and generous.

When you're focused on being "nice," you may do things just to be liked or maintain appearances such as agreeing to attend an event you don't want to go to, giving someone a fake smile or enthusiastic greeting when you really don't want anything to do with them, or not speaking up because you don't want to "rock the boat." While we may do these things to be seen as someone that others can approach and relate to, it can end up coming across as weak or insincere or not leave any type of memorable impression. As a result, the value of a "nice" person is often immeasurable or indifferent.

When you're being "kind," you genuinely care about the people around you (whether family, friends, co-workers, or strangers), communicate honestly and compassionately, and make a positive impact on the people and situations you find yourself in through supportive behavior and action. The value a "kind" person brings to the table is tangible and vital. They are the kind of people you want to have in your inner circle, on your team, and around when you find yourself in an unexpected bind.

While some actions can be nice and kind at the same time, not all nice actions are kind and not all kind actions are considered nice. Being kind means you may not do or say the things that others want to see or hear. Being kind may mean creating uncomfortable situations for the long-term good—whether for yourself, someone else, both parties, or even others affected. Being kind can also be inconvenient, go unnoticed, or lead to outcomes with some undesirable results, but living kindly requires one to live on that edge.

My Story

For me, living kindly on a consistent basis started in 2012, but it wasn't because of a commitment to kindness, it was through a personal desire to live more authentically. What I didn't realize at the time is that by following my heart, expressing my truth, and carving my own path, I was actually being kind to myself—which I've found to be the foundation for living kindly.

From leaving behind a successful six-figure corporate job at Showtime Networks, and supporting others to live more authentically through my podcast (Are You Being Real) and coaching program (Winning Weeks), I learned that by not being kind to myself, I wasn't sharing my unique perspectives and gifts, and everyone who I helped and supported during those following years would have lost out had I stuck to my comfort zone and people-pleasing ways. Furthermore, the more kind I was to myself, the more I was able to help, support, and connect with others.

Instead of questioning my role and where I fit in, I was more focused on giving, providing value, and simply being myself. In the process, I discovered that being kind to others can take an infinite number of shapes and forms and can be as simple as being a positive influence—whether lending a helping hand, sharing a laugh or smile, or making someone feel seen, heard, and valued.

This discovery blew my mind, gave me so much confidence, and became the catalyst for my life-changing daily kindness practice.

After my dad passed away in 2016, I made a post about it on social media, and I got so much love and support that I wanted to feel this loved, connected, and supported all the time and ensure others did too, so I started a daily ritual of sending personalized video messages to each of my 3,000 Facebook friends on their birthdays.

While I guessed it would be a nice gift to give and help me keep in touch, little did I know that sending appreciation videos would totally transform my life and relationships and be a gift that keeps on giving.

You see, a personalized video message (even if just 20–30 seconds) is incredibly powerful, as it really stands out from a text or generic/impersonal "happy birthday" Facebook wall post. You actually get to experience the person's voice and energy, see their face and where they are, and perhaps even see what they are doing. This creates a greater level of connection because you can feel the thoughtfulness and effort and know that the person took a few seconds out of their day to give you their kind attention (when they could be doing anything else). Because everyone feels alone or socially isolated at times, a video message can make a huge impression and literally shift someone's day in an instant.

After 12,000 LoveBomb videos and a TEDx talk, I still send personalized videos every day because I get to uplift others and experience the proven benefits of kindness!

The benefits of loving kindness:

- Increases happiness
- Decreases stress and anxiety
- Deepens connections
- Attracts more good to your life
- Instantly makes the world a brighter place

Sending the birthday videos is a gratitude practice that reminds me who I am and what I stand for every day, which amplifies the joy I feel on a good day or brightens up a dark day when things aren't going my way or when I'm not being kind to myself.

But perhaps the most special and magical part is that this daily ritual inspired me to create the LoveBomb app and a ripple effect of kindness across the world.

Nearly every day, someone tells me that I inspired them to start sending video messages, or they share a story of an interaction they had with someone that wouldn't have happened without coming across my work or the LoveBomb app. One 30-year-old man even told his dad "I love you" for the first time, and his dad replied with an equally unprecedented remark, "I love you, too."

By being kind, we not only get to help others, but experience a profound personal reward that often has a compounding effect on our lives and the world around us. If only our minds remembered this truth more often when opportunities for kindness appear!

You see, there is so much more love to go around and an infinite amount of kindness available that would aid, uplift, and unite humanity. But kind actions are often not taken, and so many kind words are left unsaid.

What's important to remember is that life is challenging, unkind influences are all around us (from the news to ads to social media), and we often never know what others are going through. As a result, if we hold back, look the other way, or just do what everybody else is doing, we rob ourselves and each other of the gift of giving and receiving support.

In a world where every person is an influencer, because we all are powerful and impact the people around us, it's important to be aware of what's influencing *us*, what *we* are influencing, and personally strive to be (what I call) a "kindfluencer."

For me, what started with self-kindness, led to a daily connection practice to uplift others, and ultimately inspired an impact—much larger than myself—that I could have only dreamed of.

This is available to anyone and everyone!

Through my unintended journey into kindness, I've discovered that being kind is rooted in three important pillars that are available to everyone in any moment: 1) being caring, 2) being helpful, and 3) being authentic.

If you approach every situation, opportunity, and person in a caring, helpful, and authentic way, you can always know that you are living kindly and coming from a place of good intention and spirit.

To best set yourself up for a life of continued kindness and impact, I recommend developing your own daily kindness practice, and encourage you to ask yourself these thought-provoking questions.

How can I be kinder to myself?

How can I be kinder to others?

How can I be kinder to the world at large?

At the end of the day, we can leave a footprint or leave a kind print. Which do you choose, and what will yours look like?

Because if not kindness, what are we influencing?

Kindhearted: How I Healed a Broken Heart

Angelica Perman

I put down the phone after I received *the dreaded text* that told me that the most amazing connection I had with another person was now over. His work demanded his full attention right now.

My body shook from deep inside, and I could feel my heart break into two pieces. One part was still with him wishing that we could be together. And the other part was me . . . on my own . . . alone in the middle of a pandemic. I had been patient. I had been kind. I had been myself. I had showed up. I had given. I had been open no matter how scared I was of getting hurt. I had been myself, the woman that he said he had been looking for . . . all his life.

But there was nothing I could say or do to convince this person that he had made a terrible mistake. He made his choice. He was not available. He shared his truth and reasons that he could not show up for the relationship. The door was left open to see me when he could. But weeks turned to months with no word. No matter how connected we had been. No matter how deep and wonderful it felt. Our time together was no more.

When this happens, to a person who is kind, generous, loyal—all the things—it is so destabilizing. What could I have done differently? Could I have given more? What did I do wrong? The feelings of helplessness swallowed me whole and spit out the dream of a future with this person.

Kind people go out of their way to bring joy, contentment, peace, healing to others, often at their own expense. I felt this kind energy between us. And plans had been made. Promises of days ahead when his schedule would open up. Intentions were created. But life and choice changed the course.

Kind and caring ones are often a magnet for those who in some way are not willing to return the kindness, and it can be viewed as selfish. A highly sensitive individual feels what other people try to hide and is sometimes willing to go to the extreme to be there for others because they know how it feels to be in deep pain. After all, they feel, well, everything. And they can sense what other people need without words.

I thought we shared this empathetic camaraderie. In the end, though, he chose himself and his path, instead of ours. I felt and thought many deep, unkind, unloving things about myself and about him after our relationship ended.

As a highly empathic woman with a private spiritual counseling and sound healing practice in Malibu, Calif., for over 20 years, I have found that every single person I've worked with, especially in addiction recovery, had the toughest time being kind to themselves. I prided myself on being open to receive and, as part of my job as a person in the field of personal growth, to give to myself. My rule is to give back to myself half of the time I spend giving to others.

The trauma of a sudden loss knocking on the sensitive soul's door and taking something they thought they would never lose can be beyond overwhelming.

Betrayal is a cruel teacher. One minute, life is filled with promises of goodness and the magic of possibility. And in an instant, the love, the hope, the life with this person is over. And all the dreams of what could be that we lived in our head are dead. A piece of our soul dies with this kind of loss. Everything you thought was one way is now done. And it can feel like a heart attack of the spirit.

And no drugs, no sex, no alcohol, no money, nor distraction can sooth the beast of aloneness that the end of a love affair has stolen right from within your chest. You walk around in a daze. How could this happen . . . again?

After I got the text, I lay on my white fluffy bed with white fluffy pillows in a white fluffy room overlooking the mountains across from my bedroom. Stunned, weeks turned to months with no word. His work was his mistress, and she had taken him from me.

I couldn't sleep. I couldn't eat. I could barely get out of bed. At the time, I was very busy working with private clients as a spiritual coach at a rehab center and in my private practice during the lockdown. I had done the impossible as my career skyrocketed, and I fell in love. To find love in a pandemic and to lose love when the world was going mad felt like the cruelest of jokes by the Universe. All this, while I worked harder than I ever had with a large and quite demanding client load.

I struggled immensely to offer high-vibe support to others, often sobbing and looking like a wreck minutes before a Facetime, Zoom call, or session at the rehab. Many times, I rolled out of bed, brushed my hair, and barely looked presentable, but somehow, I rallied to be there for my people who had lost relatives to the virus, nearly died from drugs and alcohol, suffered extreme abuse. My heartbreak seemed to pale to their extreme pain, which at times made me feel even worse.

So I did what any single, sexy, sassy, smart, and spiritual woman would do—I decided to do whatever I wanted to make myself feel better. I decided to not listen to the horrid cruel voices in my head that kept bargaining to make this love not end. The voices that said I did something wrong. That there must be something wrong with me. I made a decision to live passionately and to be kind to myself. To give to myself. To not think mean thoughts about myself. I prayed for support and love and opened myself up to other people being kind to me. It was very hard on one level—to feel so vulnerable and hurting from head to toe—but I just had to keep going.

My friends rallied around me. They listened while I cried. They massaged me and cuddled with me to give me affection. They called and texted beautiful good morning and good night messages as the absence of his deep, playful, and affectionate communication was deafening. They bought me presents. And brought me snacks. But really, it was the kindness that I allowed within that let me open up to all the kindness that was everywhere in my life.

My intention of self-kindness had little limits. I bought a new wardrobe. I got my hair done. I did daily beach walks. I fixed up my patio and room. I dated beautiful men who wanted to shower me with attention, affection, and healing. I did not want to be alone.

And I decided to allow the Universe to bring people into my life to help me heal my hurt.

The burning truth was I could not replace this person ever. I did have amazing experiences, though, and each person helped me heal and see the beauty that I embody, as well as the loveliness of my soul. And I could see the pain in their eyes too which made me feel less alone. But I did not want to get lost in another. I wanted to find myself, my new me. I pushed onward.

I journeyed with a shaman, purging my inner demons for hours into a bucket at the music studio surrounded by wonderful musical friends to get all the unbearable longing and hurt out of every single chakra. I committed myself to completing all the things I had been procrastinating on. I caught up on taxes. I completed my divorce papers. I organized my finances. While the underworld danced across my brain of all that was loveless and untrue in this life, I prevailed. I pushed through. I stood in front of my mirror and told myself how awesome I was doing. I told myself that I loved myself all day long. I did trauma release sessions. I ran head first into all that was my passion as though it were my last day on earth.

This was the only way my heart could take another day. It wasn't just that I missed him. It was the future we would never get to create that left a huge empty hole in my being. Some people cut deep. This person took one samurai sword and cut me into two people—the old me and the new me without . . . him. My broken heart left me open wide to greater gifts of creativity and spiritual abilities. Deep inside I knew this had a purpose. This could break me or make me. I chose the latter. I know he would want that for me, actually—to be self-sovereign and complete in my own self without him. His love had been pure, even if he could not be the man he had promised to be.

When I wasn't connecting with others, working, or crying, I was recording music four times a week, singing my heart out. This outlet was a lifeline. To go to the music studio in Hollywood and create songs out of the inexplicable pain I was feeling saved my life. If I could create songs that offered hope and outlets for feelings that needed to be felt, perhaps I could survive one more day. I sang about surrender. I sang about forgiveness. I sang chants about love. I sang chants about freedom and happiness. I wrote songs in my car, on my phone, in my head all day long. I sobbed in the recording booth almost uncontrollably and wasn't sure at times if I could get the lyrics out. With every part of my being, I wanted to end this pain. And I wasn't going to stop being kind to myself until the unbearable emptiness subsided.

I prayed daily for anything that could take my pain away, even if it was just for a few minutes. I jammed with my music friends singing and rocking out till all hours. I hiked. I dined. I went to hot springs. I treated myself to anything I felt like. I ate cake. But mostly, I focused on living as the best possible version of myself. Layer after layer of this heart-broken, shattered feeling started to mend. Each tear, each hug, each kind word I received, each gesture of self-love I gave to myself offered another stitch in my chest between the cracks. Like a tightrope walker, I focused on just putting one foot in front of the other over the grandest of canyons within—the hole in my spirit where the connection had been. Any misstep could lead to my doom.

I breathed deeper. I laughed harder. And I offered the most kindness to myself I could possibly extract. I went on a kindness crusade for the person who needed it the most: me. For without me, I could offer no smiles, no caring insight into the addictive patterns and trauma of my clients. I could offer no good thing to this world. Or lift anyone from their perils to higher ground. Or utter words of truth that offered a ladder of empathy to another. I could not smile at strangers. Or do any nice thing for any one of them. I could offer no light to this world without illuminating my own light and busting down the wall of denial and lack. I embraced the one true thing I could.

I went even deeper. I looked inside at all my anxious avoidant ways I had been in relationships. How I wanted closeness, sometimes at the expense of what was good for my mental wellbeing. And how I had been the runner too. How I put up a wall of pleasantness, pleasure seeking, and bravery to hide my deep fear of abandonment. And I realized I had been too patient and understanding at my own expense. Making excuses for the other person. For many people. And not being truly kind to myself. By making it easy on them, I had made it hard on me. And I had put my own needs on the back burner. Lying to myself that they would come around. Believing promises that never happened. And this was not loving to myself and did them a disservice as well. It made it so I was waiting on them. Their schedule. Their availability.

But when your heart is broken, it can be hard to do anything, even to take your next breath feels like too much effort.

The medicine that healed me of the deepest loss I have felt was that I had to tell myself the truth and live it. To be kind to myself. Be real. Show up full on for me, not just for everyone else. Don't make excuses. Don't ever give up on my own dreams even if another has.

And be kind to this sacred heart of gold I have in my own hands. Be kindhearted and know that I will love again . . .

Until then, I promised to love the shit out of myself with all of me. To trust that my needs are important enough to be my top priority. To no longer play second to anyone else. No work mistress. No man. No old belief in my head.

In my search for relief, I had found the one thing I could count on when others let me down, disappeared, ghosted, lacked integrity— that I am kindhearted to the core. And all the kindness I have generated toward others I needed to give to myself like an endless fountain of light.

Love came to me to heal me. Not the beloved I craved and missed terribly. Not the one who did not return. But from the one person who could love me unconditionally. Myself. I learned what love is: to be kind to yourself is the first and absolutely most important step to being an emissary of kindness on this planet. To thy own self be true, and the ones who are meant for you shall come. They will hear your call. And because they are kind to themselves too, they will know that you are a part of them and they are a part of you.

The ones who walked away? They couldn't be kind to you, not in the way that you wanted or deserved because they weren't being kind to themselves. Walking away from love is the exact opposite of being kind to the self. And if that person does come back to love again, perhaps there could still be another chapter, but I won't wait or hold my breath. I now walk with my full, tenacious, fully expressed self, committed fully to giving myself loving kindness. And I will unite with those who have the kindness code etched on their heart.

Under all the armor and scar tissue from all the broken pieces of hurt, abandonment, trauma, and pain that I endured, I now know that being kind to me is what true love is. And for this I am grateful. My broken heart was a teacher and taught me well.

And now, I live with the following tenet in all my relationships to make sure I don't lose myself again. When I think thoughts about myself or others that could bring me down into the spiral of suffering, I ask myself:

Are these thoughts kind? Are these thoughts true? Are these thoughts necessary?

I healed my broken heart by being kind to myself and being open to love again . . .

And love has found me. Love is everywhere. Love is inside my kind heart.

Living Kindly

Micro-Moments, Massive Impact

Jonathan Darling

"I'm sorry sir. Your card has been declined."

Those words echoed in my ears so loudly that I wanted to ask the cashier to please not shout at me. What was I going to do?

I stood there, looking up at the green lights that illuminated the screen.

$114.56

I looked back down at the debit card she had handed back to me.

I looked back up at the total.

"Can you run it again please?" I asked.

"I'm really sorry, sir," the cashier stated. "I ran it twice now. Do you have another card you can use?"

I didn't.

I was a junior at Ball State University and had just got back into Muncie, Ind., from traveling home for Christmas break. I had stopped at the local Walmart to buy groceries for my apartment and some supplies that I needed for the start of school. As usual, Walmart was packed with people, everyone trying to check out at the exact same time, and there were only two cashier lanes open.

As I stood there, looking at my load of groceries, now knowing that I didn't have enough money in my bank account to pay for everything, I was lost. What would I return? Could I take back some of the food and make it until my next paycheck? Should I just take back some of the school supplies?

I could feel the eyes of what felt like the entire population of Muncie staring at me. I could sense impatience growing with the customers behind me as they started to mumble and groan with displeasure. I was paralyzed. Every part of me wanted to drop everything, cover my head with a brown grocery sack, and run as fast as I could out of the store, but I couldn't move.

As I stood there, the lady behind me in line walked around her grocery cart toward me. I figured she had gotten tired of watching me become a statue and decided to abandon ship. As she moved closer, I lowered my head in shame, hoping that we wouldn't make eye contact. Then I felt a hand on my shoulder. I looked up and saw her handing her credit card to the cashier.

"Oh please no ma'am . . . please don't," I whispered. "I'll just take some of this stuff back. I'm so sorry I'm keeping you waiting."

She looked up at me and smiled. "We have all been there. We have all needed a little help now and then." She patted me on the back and said, "I'm glad I could be here to help."

With tears flowing down my face, I hugged her and thanked her. I had never had anyone, let alone a stranger, do anything like that for me EVER! I was blown away, incredibly grateful and completely and utterly confused. Why would anyone do that for someone? It was such a small moment. Yet a momentary interaction at Walmart made a massive impact in my life.

I had just experienced my first random act of kindness.

That moment changed my life forever. It gave me incredible hope that there are still good people in this world, people who have incredible hearts and who care for those around them. That moment inspired me to become more vigilant, watching for opportunities to pay it forward.

After that day, I experienced many more moments like that. Some of these moments happened to me, others were opportunities where I created the moment. I began seeing opportunities to care for people every day, in almost any environment I was in. What I realized was that, the more intentional I was, the more "random acts" I had the opportunity to do.

That's when it hit me. Maybe these moments weren't random. Maybe I just hadn't been paying attention. How many of these moments was I missing every single day by just not being present or intentional in my interactions?

I want you to close your eyes for a moment.

I want you to think about a typical day. Specifically, I want you to think about how many people you interact with on any given day from the moment you wake up. Think about the interactions with your family, your neighbors, the people in line at your local coffee shop. Then I want you to think about the strangers you pass on the street, your coworkers. Think about the conversations with your friends.

Now open your eyes.

Recently on social media, I asked the following question to my friends and connections:

"How many people do you have a face-to-face moment with on any given day?"

The answers I received ranged from five to hundreds. They stated that it depended on their day and whether or not they were at work or out running errands. I decided to clarify the question a little more, digging a little deeper, by defining an interaction as a smile or a verbal exchange. The numbers remained the same. Whether it was with a stranger or a close companion, these small interactions are happing to everyone. Not a single person responded with the answer "zero." Everyone, every day, had a small interaction with another human being.

I decided to define these interactions as Micro-Moments. These Micro-Moments are the small, very brief periods of interaction we have with other people. These Micro-Moments could be a smile to a stranger, a conversation while in line at the grocery store, or a passing word between coworkers in the hall. If you engage with another human, whether it is visually, verbally, or physically, you are having a Micro-Moment. When I calculated the amount of Micro-Moments we have on a daily basis, the numbers were staggering.

Let's just say that, on average, we experience ten interactions with other people every single day. That means, in one week's time, we have a total of 70 Micro-Moments. That equals 304 Micro-Moments per month and a total of 3,650 micro-moments per year.

I know what you are probably thinking: "So what?" "What is so important about these Micro-Moments?"

What's important is that each one of these Micro-Moments is an opportunity to make a *massive impact* in the lives of those people we are interacting with.

Now before you start freaking out about the word "massive," I'm not talking about the size of the action you take in that moment. It's not about grandness, but about the intent.

The Massive part comes from the idea that you can completely change the trajectory of someone's day or life with something as small as a smile or a kind word. Each one of these Micro-Moments becomes opportunities for us to leave someone else's life a little better because we were there.

But before we go any farther, can I get something off of my chest?

By now you are probably thinking that these Micro-Moments sound an awful lot like random acts of kindness, and in theory, I can completely see the correlation.

But I'm going to be very blunt . . .

And this might sting a little . . .

Why have we relegated kindness to a "random act" instead of an intentional way we choose to live our life?

Have our lives, schedules, and personal priorities become so important that we have to set aside kindness and make it something we seldom do? When did we become so self-centered that the idea of being kind to others is "random"? The bigger question is that if we are only being "randomly" kind, to "random people," then what the hell are we being to everyone else the rest of the time? (Just turn on the TV or look through social media, and you will be able to answer that last question pretty easily.)

We have to get past the mentality of kindness being random and embrace the idea that there are endless opportunities to make a massive, positive impact on the world around us by taking advantage of the Micro-Moments we are given every day. It's about becoming intentional in these moments, paying attention to the areas where we can lean in and lift up those around us.

While this might be an overwhelming thought, the impact we can make in these micro-moments not only changes the lives of those around us but ultimately changes the world.

That's right, *the world*!

One of my favorite quotes is by Mother Teresa. She said, "I alone cannot change the world, but I can cast a stone across the waters to create many ripples." When you understand that these Micro-Moments can have a massive impact in the lives of others, you are casting the stone and creating the ripples. You inspire those around you and those who have been impacted by you to go out and do the same. What might look like a small ripple at your local Starbucks, could grow into a great tsunami, changing the lives of millions across the globe.

The question is . . .

Are you willing to cast the first stone?

Living Kindly

The Lessons of Living Kindly

Leigh M. Clark

So kindness really is all around us—within us, in the hearts of those we touch with our compassion and love, in caring for animals and our planet.

We've learned that kindness can be as simple as loving yourself before you can give to the world around you, having an intentional mindset to do good in each of our experiences, simply showing compassion, or spending less than $10 on a gesture to a stranger we'd like to surprise. At the core of it, it's giving a piece of ourselves, maybe even a big piece of ourselves like saving a life through donating an organ. At the heart of kindness is intention to do something to put something positive into a world that needs that energy to continue to thrive.

No matter how simple or grand the act is, with each moment of positivity we exude, we are changing the balance of the energy and balancing out the negative that threatens to overwhelm each of us, around the globe.

You heard at the beginning of this book how one act of kindness was a drop that became a ripple, that became a wave, that's now shifting the world. You're a part of this movement just by reading the heartfelt stories that our authors have shared with good intent and a desire to make a difference.

Perhaps you were moved to take action, or maybe you shed a tear when reading the levels of compassion people can find within themselves to pass along to the next, each moment collected creating a multiplicity that placed these words in front of you.

The most important thing to take from this collection of perspectives on kindness is that even your words can leave an indelible mark on the souls of others. Being vulnerable enough to share our thoughts and experiences is a gesture of kindness, and we hope that they continue to be paid forward through the moments you create from this day forward or from the stories you will share of moments that have inspired you.

It's important that we think back on the essays you've experienced in Living Kindly and truly discern what the lasting message of their individual and collective stories have demonstrated.

We started this book with the motivation to bring this into existence and the wild way it all started in 2012 with one simple act. The connections, stories and experiences that emerged from that first small step shifted one person into touching the lives of countless others.

We learned that kindness can change a frown to a smile, even if for a fleeting moment. A story of a holiday act that became a national endeavor, and a story of how fleeting life is and how everyone just wants to be seen and appreciated.

The stories that I shared have shaped my heart into something bigger and brighter than I ever knew was possible. It led me to others who shared their stories with me, and in turn, with you.

We heard from **Neil Schambra Stevens** in Amsterdam who showed us that Kindness inspires real change in the workplace.

He illustrated that when you are intentional with kindness, it creates a mindset that everybody embraces throughout the organization, and that's when true transformational change happens.

Kindness is the secret sauce and rocket fuel for both people and business.

Neil experienced a touching moment that shifted his perspective on what living your legacy truly means.

He wants you to know that he would like to be remembered as someone who supported people being seen, heard, and valued.

He hopes his chapter leaves you to ponder what you would like to be remembered for.

Life is fragile but the mark you leave lives on.

When I stepped off the stage of the Working Women of Tampa Bay's Annual Conference, having just delivered a speech about finding my purpose through kindness, a small group of women was waiting there, looking to share their thoughts on what I'd presented.

I never rehearsed because I always want to have sincere conversations with the audience in front of me and have that human exchange rather than what I had perfected. However the previous night, I knew I needed to mentally prep, so I watched a stream of TED talks and thought about the impact of delivery, rather than my story, which I had already lived and was an expert on.

One of the women in that line was **Beth Socoski**, and she asked me if I'd be interested in doing a TED talk, she had instantly and inherently known that I sincerely believed in the value of kindness. I would later learn that this was a huge part of who she was at her core.

Beth and I got to know each other, and I realized what a unicorn of kindness she truly was. Aside from her busy career, she helped out multiple charities and even ran one herself. She showed me how she found ways to give back no matter the effort.

I was thrilled when, a year later, she agreed to be part of this collective. I knew she had so much wisdom to share with our readers.

Some of the lessons her chapter called out include the importance of reaching out. You can be the greatest, kindest, and most giving person, but you need to cast your thread out onto the world.

it is 110% OK if something doesn't work out or fit for you. That's life, learning, and growing.

Embrace it, gain from it, and move on to the next great adventure. And most importantly, Your actions will impact the world around you in ways you aren't even aware of yet. Go out, and do good.

Next we heard from **Cori Wamsley** in Pittsburgh, Pennsylvania, who examined her ever-changing perspective on kindness, especially when illustrating it to her children and helping to shape their own perceptions of being kind and how to be heart led.

When I asked her what she wants to remain with you from the words she penned, she wants to ensure that we know it's possible to fear or be suspicious of kindness, but owning your power and trusting yourself helps you experience true kindness in full and more often.

In terms of how her view on kindness has evolved, she wants to remind us that our definition of "kindness" may change as we grow, but we need to know what it is for ourselves, why we do it, and how it feels inside to know that we are making the most impact with what we give.

Most importantly she knows inherently in her examination and experiences with kindness that we have the power to change the planet with each generation as we learn to accept, embrace, and pass on true kindness.

Next we heard from the badass in Texas, **Jo Davis**, who allows us to understand the grit that comes with being authentic in how we approach living kindly. It is evident within her passionate perspective that kindness doesn't need to be graceful and pretty. It can be raw, real, and messy.

While impulsivity often gets a bad rap, we should act intuitively and for our highest levels of true joy without overthinking it. What happens when we simply ACT on the impulse to do what feels right and kind without concern for gratitude? It always serves the highest good. It also makes you kind of a badass, because you are walking in your truth and allowing the best parts of life to emerge.

Next we heard from **Francesca Donlan** in Southwest Florida who brought her whole class, with their permission slips, to share lessons with you. I've personally been a guest lecturer for her course in kindness at FGCU, and I've seen firsthand these students present on the acts of kindness they come up with through the course.

Hearing their experiences is so heartwarming because they haven't yet been jaded by a sometimes cruel world, and many have not realized how they can really affect the hearts and minds of others. Kindness is the greatest teacher. (Francesca is pretty amazing too!)

One night when I was a guest lecturer at her university, the students kept me after class to ask some additional questions. One student said: "Do you get validation from your number of followers?"—a question that seemed so aligned with their generation where even your inspiration could be measured by the audience size.

I paused and began, "I started all of this to make an impact, so of course, seeing metrics that confirm that's happening is nice. However, it's moments like this—talking to all of you—that mean more to me than thousands of fleeting connections online."

I knew that night they had all learned something about how dreams are realized not by likes, or followers, or views. They were able to see a clear example that shining your light just to help others will, in turn, radiate back onto you, so long as giving the light to others was without agenda or expectation. They knew that if you stepped into your purpose, the world would truly be inspired.

In summarizing her chapter, I want to be sure to speak to the lesson that I took from each student's story. I hope they are reading this book, sharing it with their friends and loved ones. And, if you are one of these students, I'm standing and applauding. You are all the future, the legacies we exchange to you are yours to continue to innovate and grow upon. Make them uniquely yours, and use your passion for the greater good. As Francesca said to me, "Kindness is a way of spreading hope of a new future."

Wiktoria shares that she will always remember to do something nice and unexpected because kindness gave her a feeling of euphoria that was derived from doing something unexpected for someone else.

Guadalupe found in her act of kindness that she recognized the loneliness that losing a loved one created for her and her father. Instead of thinking only of her own feelings, she decided to honor others who had passed by decorating the graves that looked lonely and without visitors at the cemetery. It is truly uplifting to see that she was empathetic to those who could not be with their loved ones, both living and those who had passed. It reminds me that kindness is eternal, and it is a way to honor the past and the present.

Emma shares her experience bringing the crafts she did with her grandma before the dementia set in. She brought a loving gesture to the memory care facility by way of vases and silk flowers. Her story reminds me how the simplest act of realizing what may spark joy in others is born out of being considerate and empathetic to what stage they were experiencing in their lives.

We've heard of pay it forward drive-through lines, Savannah went a route even more compassionate than just an act of kindness; she did an act of consideration when she saw the driver behind her in tears. It prompted her to buy the order for them. I can only imagine how much that meant to someone having a bad day. That's such a testament to recognizing the struggles that others face. That is even more important than the coffee alone.

Nick shares about his experience caring for animals at the sanctuary he worked at and bringing them special treats. I love this perspective because so often we think of human kindness, but including animals and nature is so special. This is an opportunity to help creatures that cannot always control their outcomes and rely on others to care for them. When we can see that as an opportunity for compassion, giving is a beautiful thing.

Stormy decided to buy some treats for a lonely neighbor, and that has since sparked a friendship. The gesture she did for one moment created a bond between her and her elderly neighbor. She has since begun to visit her frequently. That is the lesson that his story illustrated to me: sometimes just having company is more than enough for so many lonely souls.

Ariandne encountered something most of us fear, which is that an unexpected act of kindness will be rejected. However the outcome was even more special. Although the gentleman she tried to pay it forward to declined her gift, he let her know that the gesture was more important than the gift. She learned a lesson that sometimes life can harden our hearts, but someone reaching out to let you know they see you and wish you joy is enough to restore their faith in humanity.

Francesca will continue to lead and inspire the next generation, and for each of those students reading, thank you for reminding us all how much kindness can change the future.

Magnus Wood, from across the pond in England, shares a moving story of kindness, fitting because kindness is his business and he understands better than most how kindness can move the immovable and is the line that connects most dots. He shares a story that we've all experienced, being in a job that's created burnout, and how sometimes at extremes this can affect our health, leaving us with dis-ease as well as actual disease. Moreover, there's a slow death of the lives full of purpose we had thought we would lead, when we trade our happiness for material wealth.

I was told something once, that Magnus' chapter reminds me of. We all start out thinking of the ultimate happiness we can achieve, and as we let our dreams begin to collect dust, in favor of taking the path that seems predictably safe for financial reasons alone, we may eventually meet ourselves at the intersection where we are financially comfortable and wonder how we got so far off course.

The path to happiness is often the one the majority of us don't take; we instead take the safe route, which is where our life's adventure detours into the mundane.

The quote that really caught me among Magnus' words was that the most common regret of the dying is, "I wish I'd had the courage to live a life true to myself, not the life others expected of me." Did you feel like that hit you sideways? I know I did. I made a change years ago in the direction of combining the safe route with a dedication to find joy in giving back, and people balked at the time.

"Won't your employer think you doing this charity will take away from your productivity?"

I found one that believed in my heart and believed giving back was good for their employees.

"Well what if you lose that one?"

I found another one with an even bigger organization that was equally supportive.

We often tell ourselves that being happy and being wealthy is a decision we have to choose between. These two principles should be intertwined because happiness is a form of wealth. It's emotional currency. When you're happy and thriving in your purpose, more people want to work alongside that kind of energy. It's not one or the other. It's both.

These are some of the lessons that chapter gave to me. Magnus wants to be sure that you take these lessons with you as well:

Be kind to yourself—because kindness starts with you.

Be kind to others—because we are all interconnected.

Be kind to the planet—because the future of humanity and all life on Earth depends on us.

But, more than anything . . . you know you feel it. The call of kindness. Don't refuse the call.

Next we heard from **Cole Baker Bagwell** who is in Raleigh, North Carolina. From the moment I met Cole through that fateful LinkedIn search, I knew I had stumbled on an enigma. What I loved the most about Cole's contribution was how effortlessly she could simplify the core of kindness. She had told me from our earliest conversations that she lived by the principal of "do no harm."

I wasn't quite sure what she meant, but like those who read her story, it really is that easy.

Kindness can be as simple as a mindset, a way of approaching the moments of your life. An attitude that focuses on leaving each situation no worse than where you found it is the baseline of using a kind heart in the way you carry out your life.

Actions speak louder than words, but words have a significant weight as well. Often we get caught up in stressful conversations or, worse, gossip, and we feel entitled, that we deserve to have our resentments or judgements towards others.

What Cole illustrates is that the simple approach that you will not worsen a situation with your words and/or actions allows for you to assess what you are bringing to these moments.

This reminds me of the old saying:

Is it true?

Is it kind?

Is it necessary?

What if we each took the task to own our emotional experiences and refuse to increase negativity by matching it with our own?

I also love that she challenged the idea of random acts of kindness. At first, I felt defensive because I built a movement on random acts of kindness. They are what began my passion to give back. However, I have a hard and fast rule that, if I am defensive about something, there is some truth in it. Otherwise why would it trigger me?

So I gave it deeper examination and realized that what she means is by saying it's "random," we actually sell the kindness short. Claiming it was an aimless gesture proves there was no thoughtful intention behind it. After realizing this, I've decided I agree with her.

Kindness is never random; it is thoughtful, empathetic, purposeful. It's the decision to do the right thing, or the kind thing, or just something to put goodness into the situation however we can.

It goes back to her overarching theme of do no harm. The mindset alone is the biggest action we need to take in every situation. Be a helper—think *how can I help here?* Or better yet, ask someone in need what you can do to help. A lot of the time, genuine listening is all they really need.

Cole wants to ensure you left her chapter with two very important points. 1) Kindness innately marries the heart with the mind—a force for good that's contagious.

And above all else, 2) redefining kindness as a commitment to do no harm (to leave everyone and everything better) and letting that guide our thoughts, words, and actions, has the power to positively transform us and the world we share.

Next we heard from **Debbie Lundberg** in Tampa, who did an unbelievably selfless act of kindness by choosing to give life to another human by way of giving a piece of her heart and one of her kidneys.

I can say I've known Debbie a little over two years, mostly before she did this courageous act, and she continues to impress me with how her words and her actions are aligned. She truly lives her life in a way that lights the spirits of so many others; she inspires in the way she approaches each day of her life.

I'm fairly certain her story leaves a lasting impression, but some of the things she hopes that you take from it include:

A kind act for the sake of attention is showmanship. A kind act for the sake of engaging financially is business. A kind act for the sake of true connection with, and positive impact on, another person is KINDNESS!

Kindness takes little to no money, yet an abundance of security, interest, and desire to have a positive outcome beyond self (while including oneself in the positivity) is never discouraged. It's the joy that emerges from the experience that is the true treasure.

Also she wants you to leave her chapter knowing that thinking about kindness is a wonderful idea, while acting on kindness creates wonderful energy. That energy is usually felt by the giver and the recipient as well.

Most importantly, a single act of kindness can be the foundation for a lifetime of kind thoughts, actions, and outcomes!

It is never too early, or too late, to be kind.

Daniel Levin is one of the first authors I met—before the book was even a vision. He had me on his podcast, The Mosaic, and I knew I had found one incredibly insightful and sincere human. He had another podcast as well, which is all about conversations with strangers, which has no scripting or prep ahead. He explained to me the wonderful magnetic dialogue he shared with people from all walks of life. I realized this man had an invaluable gift, he not only could hear what you were saying, but he was capable of being an intent listener.

In a world today where people often listen to respond rather than listening to learn, this was so refreshing. We struck up a friendship, and when I learned more about his story, I knew he had to be one of the first I'd ask to participate in this project.

In Daniel's chapter, he shares some of these incredible stories he had shared with me, but also so many I'd never heard. Although Daniel has an incredible gift for listening, it's even more endearing to hear him speak because when he speaks, he tells you what he's learned while listening.

When I walk into a room, I know every moment that I had experienced prior to that, so when I listen instead of speaking, I leave with even more experiences than I could collect on my own.

In Daniel's first story, he tells a beautiful story of the power of non-verbal communication when he had a breakthrough with one of the great loves of his life, his daughter. When he told me this story, I had chills. How many parents, like myself, feel they cannot always understand what their kids are trying to communicate?

However, Danny's story reminds me how often we aren't listening. They are telling us in their way; we just want to hear it in the way we are used to. Such a testimony to life, how we go about our days feeling we don't understand others because we want them to communicate the way we do. We are not asking for a conversation, perhaps only a mirror. How can we learn from that?

Daniel's stories continue to challenge us to look at the communication of the heart over our own opinions, the power of giving someone our time in exchange for their stories and allowing them the privilege to be really heard.

I hope his stories impact you as much as they have impacted me.

When I asked Daniel what he wanted the readers to remember, I listened very carefully.

Everyone wants three things, to be loved and accepted, listened to and heard, acknowledged and validated, and that is something we can give to all people. So make it your intention to do this for at least one person every day.

Everything is speaking to us—our bodies are talking to us, our businesses are talking to us, and even our environment is talking to us. If you take the time to listen to what it is saying to you, life will have much less conflict.

In closing Daniel's section, take 10 minutes to go up to someone you do not know, ask them how they are doing, and then just listen to them. Do not try to help them, fix them, change them, or tell them what to do. Just listen to them. In the course of a life, everyone can find 10 minutes.

When I met **Krystle Mabery**, she had just begun to find her way into giving back and asked if I could help her with ways to get involved. When I checked in with her periodically, and when this book was in the works, I found that those initial small acts of kindness had turned into a pursuit to continue in philanthropy through her consulting and professional career.

Her story, like mine, began with a pivotal point in her career that left her wondering more about her true purpose. When she began one holiday season with a few small acts of kindness, it continued to uplift her spirit, creating a driving force to center her life on giving back and getting involved in every way she can.

Watching her kindness journey has been so special, and it took me back to the moment a single drop of kindness started to pool. She was enlightened that she needed to find a way to live a life to inspire her soul and, in turn, the lives of those she affected.

The lessons she has taken from this journey thus far, that she hopes you'll glean from her story, are simple and yet profound. Being kind to ourselves fuels us to be kind to those around us. Letting ourselves define kindness by just taking on workload doesn't equate to true compassion. It equates to performance.

Kindness begins exactly where we are. This is one of my biggest takeaways from her chapter. That sometimes we look for opportunity to find us, instead of seeking it out. When we identify that we want to give, we can start where we are. We can use what resource we have, be it our time, talent or treasure to help someone else in this world. We don't necessarily need to take on the whole staircase but just take that first step and keep going from there.

Lastly, a very important lesson here is how powerful your presence is. Be fully in the moment with others, get involved, and share your voice, vision, and perspective. Maybe call someone who may be struggling and offer them just your energy and your light. Even as we saw in the previous chapter we can merely listen, and that is so powerful.

With the power of technology, we can video chat, send a text or a gif or a meme to someone, but maybe go old school and send them a card. Again intention is the first step in kindness.

When **Mark Shapiro** appeared in my Linkedin search on kindness, I was intrigued by his kind business and what he had done to make kindness into a digital skill as well as a personal philosophy.

One of the things that struck me during our initial conversation was how kindness was embedded into every fiber of his being, his business endeavors, and his message to the world. Like many of us, facing a personal turning point through loss, he was able to turn that into something that would drive goodness, rather than wallowing in sadness.

The lesson on the difference between being nice and being kind was particularly impactful. Many of us think that being nice is being kind. He points out that being nice can be a means to a personality trait, to be pleasant and to "get along" with others, even in some cases a way to avoid conflict.

Whereas being kind is action-driven and internally motivated. Again the intention theme has run throughout this book. Kindness is an intentional action to meet a human or worldly need. To be of service and to do so without expecting anything in return.

I really love the concept he brought to reality in the LoveBomb app because it allows people to interact with others to intentionally brighten their day with "love bombs." Those small moments create something meaningful in connecting with others and being present.

He's studied kindness at great lengths through his own journey, his kindness company Digital Humanity, and tons of research.

What he's learned through this pursuit to make an impact is that loving kindness toward others can produce a sense of well-being within yourself. Many people choose to use mood altering substances to achieve happiness, decrease stress and anxiety, or have more fun in their lives. But these are just chemicals that change our happiness. Or perhaps it's other dopamine enhancing vices like shopping, food, and so on. We are all looking for something to change how we feel.

Many of the things that people are seeking can be found through the simplicity of practicing kindness. It's also something that changes the mood of others in many cases, not just in yourself alone.

By being thoughtful in the way we approach kindness, we allow for meaningful interactions and outcomes.

Mark has made a career of accelerating kindness and ensuring it can be something both thoughtful and easy—and meaningful at its core.

Next we met another intuitive soul, **Angelica Perman** in California, who shared her vulnerable truth of how in our most painful moments we can go inward. When we allow ourselves the opportunity to truly feel our feelings, it is kindness to ourselves and restores our ability to shine our lights on the world, even when we face darkness.

She shares how a common suffering most of us can relate to is the sting of a broken heart that can leave us feeling completely depleted. Angelica shared through her sage wisdom that heartbreak can be an opportunity to take the hurt and tremendous pain to fuel you to treat yourself more kindly.

Many of us have felt abandoned at some point in our lives by someone we trusted who can't be there to support our individual journey. Kindness gives us the strength to carry on and find a place inside to grow into a stronger and brighter version of ourselves.

It's been said that sometimes we need the cracks in our journeys to allow the light to shine in and, in turn, radiate that light outward.

Jonathan Darling is from another LinkedIn search that led me to an amazing human. From the moment I interacted with him, we had the same vision on impact through kindness. His sincerity and humility made him someone I knew our readers would learn from.

His concept of Micro-Moments leading to massive impact is one that I've already incorporated into my daily existence. I seek now to act in these moments, collect these moments, and exchange these moments with others.

Through Jonathan's chapter, I learned that there are multiple opportunities, every single day, to make a massive impact in someone's life through being intentional in our Micro-Moments of interaction.

Again he took a stance on random acts of kindness as not a happenstance but rather a way of life that carries through each day.

Massive impact is not based on the size of the action, but on the sincerity of heart in the moment. A smile, encouraging word, or a pat on the back are all small actions that can make a massive impact in someone's day.

When you adopt this mindset, you're instantly more mindful of what's happening throughout each day. The moment we hurry through the line at the store on our cell phones, rushing, never looking up at the cashier. Missed moment. The moment we walk by someone down on their luck on the street and look away as to not contribute is an opportunity to contribute a smile or a look of acknowledgement on their human experience. We need to look up, be present, and see all of the magic in moments that often escape us because we are just not paying attention to how those Micro-Moments become the collection that's the massive impact upon your life and those you are able to interact with. Stop for a moment and collect those exchanges; your awareness is sometimes more than enough, if not for you—for those you see.

The lesson I take the most from Living Kindly is that as long as you hope to have a kind life, you can find one, and the positivity will multiply in time. It doesn't matter how much kindness you exhibit, or your resources, it just matters that you are thoughtful about it and find ways—however small—to take action.

From personal experience, I can tell you that my kindness journey has provided an immeasurable amount of joy. When I began, I felt lost in my life and felt everything was happening *to* me and not *for* me. I felt like I didn't know where I was headed.

But moment by moment, one act of kindness at a time, something began to spark joy in my life and drive a renewed sense of direction.

One of the most rewarding kind moments I've had in this lifetime is learning about each of these individuals and being able to share them with the rest of the world.

Kindness is being motivated by your heart to find better within yourself, to find better within others, and ultimately to lead a life that you can leave behind as a legacy. It's important that we collect these moments, and that we think about the people who we interact with each day.

In a world that's been overturned by negativity, division, disease, and financial turmoil, now more than ever, we need to be the change. We don't need to look down on anyone, or judge them. Rather we should know that each of us is fighting our own hard battle. We could all use a kind gesture or at least an acknowledgment, a smile, and basic humanity.

If somebody has fallen down, we need to give them a hand up. When we fall down, we need to ask for help.

In the years since I started that one small act of kindness, I have seen the magnificence of multiplicity that can happen when you're willing to speak up and advocate. If you have nothing else, you always have your voice, your intentions, and your energy that you can give to people.

I fully believe that our energy is the most valuable thing that we will ever possess. If you notice in the Kindleigh and Kindness Community logos there's a little "+" right at the top left of the logo. That + sign is a reminder to have a positive charge because the world is full of negative charge from those who can't help but have that energy within them. There are also those who are neutral, trying to stay quiet and not expend energy. Sometimes that is merely people just trying to hold on.

If we bring our best energy; the most we can muster into each and every day, we have the potential to change the world. I have seen in less than a decade the opportunity to take one act of kindness and turn it into a movement that's now landed in your hands.

I take this moment with you to say, "You have enough. You are enough." Go be enough, and show your goodness. As the expression goes, the only person you ever need to be better than is the person you were yesterday. Sometimes that means going inward, and that's perfectly fine because the world needs your good energy.

I hope you are as inspired as I am from hearing from these authors and the lives they've impacted or witnessed. If you're reading this, you've already made a difference. A portion of each book sale, both digital and paperback, will go to Kindleigh Inc. From these proceeds, we plan to have the team carry out unique acts of kindness. This will be the first time our organization's acts of kindness will be performed globally. You are making that happen alongside us.

Beyond that, you've helped create an energy and a life that's more positive. Appreciate the people who surround you, the opportunities and the lifetime you've been afforded. Find the strength from within to give your good energy to those around you.

We appreciate you taking time to learn about everyone in this book and paying it forward by forwarding it to a friend or sharing the stories within it. When you do your own acts of kindness, let us know by adding a #livingkindly and posting about them. It will be wonderful for us all to experience the power these words carry forth.

With kindness, the light comes from within you and radiates to those you encounter. In turn, it can help them radiate their light onto the people they encounter. And then, the world becomes more illuminated with positive energy.

Together, we can make the world a kinder place . . . one act of kindness at a time.

About the Authors

Leigh M. Clark

Illuminating the World with Kindness

Leigh M. Clark is on a mission to make an impact. From her busy career transforming businesses through technology, to her charity that throws around kindness like confetti, everything Clark works at is about making a difference.

Her nonprofit Kindleigh has made a significant impact nationwide in efforts such as gathering school supplies for foster children, distributing crucial items to the homeless, delivering gifts to women and children who are victims of abuse and human trafficking, and paying off holiday layaways for strangers. Their work has been featured on *Rachael Ray*, *The Today Show*, and many other national media outlets.

Her hope is to inspire others to live their best life by sharing their own positivity. She believes that we can make the world a nicer place, one act of kindness at a time. Through helping to uplift others she has found her purpose and is leaving an indelible mark.

Connect with Leigh:

www.kindleigh.org

www.facebook.com/groups/kindnesscommunity

www.instagram.com/kindleigh_org/

www.linkedin.com/groups/12519221

www.linkedin.com/in/leighmc

www.facebook.com/leighmclark

www.instagram.com/leigh.m.clark/

Neil Schambra Stevens

Shining the Light: Living a Legacy of Kindness

Neil Schambra Stevens is a founder, advisor, and people strategist focusing on well-being and productivity in the workplace, especially for the next generation of leadership.

He draws on over 20 years' experience as a CMO/VP with Fortune 500 brands and corporations, including Converse, Vans, Levi's, and Polaroid.

This experience has highlighted the importance of putting "People First" and encouraging them to be their best selves, both individually and collectively as a team.

He works with brands, agencies, and companies to bring a fresh mindset to work around kindness. He supports future-facing organizations to create ways of working that are more human-centric in essence. Balancing well-being and productivity is simply a better way of working for people, product, and planet. He believes kindness is the #1 piece to unlock in business to grow your people and your business.

His definition of "kindness" is enabling people to be seen, to be heard, and to be valued and has created bespoke programs and strategies to enable leaders to achieve this, especially whilst working remotely.

He enables this through practices in kindness, gratitude, momentum, and resilience, which are the founding principles of Mercury Jam, his business consultancy.

Originally from the U.K., his career path has enabled him to collect life and work experiences along the way across Europe, Asia, and the U.S.

Neil believes in simplicity and encourages the principle of "Working From Anywhere," and currently lives in and runs Mercury Jam from a houseboat in Amsterdam.

Connect with Neil:

www.mercuryjam.com/

www.instagram.com/mercury_jam/

nl.linkedin.com/company/mercury-jam

Beth Socoski

Weaving A Web of Kindness

Beth believes that we all have the ability to make a difference and that everyone should.

By day she works in the healthcare industry and devotes her time to helping and inspiring others. She is the curator and host of TEDxWestshore, the board vice president of Tampa Crossroads, the board chair of the American Lung Association in Tampa Bay, and an award-winning Meals on Wheels volunteer, and she runs her own small nonprofit focusing on community education and helping bring awareness to other organizations doing good in the world.

Beth has an M.S.W. from the University of Pittsburgh, an M.B.A. from Waynesburg University, and an M.S.C.L. from Duquesne University.

Cori Wamsley

Kindness from Ground Zero

Cori Wamsley, CEO of Aurora Corialis Publishing, works with ambitious professionals who have a transformational story to share. She helps them quickly and easily write and publish a book for their brand that helps them be seen as an expert while building a relationship with the reader.

Cori's process helps them avoid the stress of not knowing what to write, writing for the wrong audience, or telling stories that don't click with the reader, while trying to figure out the whole publishing process and run their business or nonprofit at the same time. She helps her clients reach their next level of leadership with a book, gain unshakeable confidence in their authority, and earn a massive feather in their cap by becoming a bestselling author.

Cori's bestselling book *The SPARK Method: How to Write a Book for Your Business Fast* and her unique publishing programs empower leaders to get their message heard.

Cori has 16 years' experience as a professional writer and editor, including 10 years with the U.S. Department of Energy and U.S. Department of Justice and four years as the executive editor of *Inspiring Lives Magazine*. She also wrote seven fiction books, including the children's book *Monkey Mermaid Magic*, which she coauthored with her daughter London and also illustrated. She contributed chapters to the anthologies *Twenty Won* and *Living Kindly*. Cori holds a master's and bachelor's in English literature (and a random bachelor's in biology).

She lives in Pittsburgh, Pa., with her husband and two daughters.

Connect with Cori:

www.coriwamsley.com

www.linkedin.com/in/cori-wamsley

www.facebook.com/CoriWamsley

www.instagram.com/coriwamsley

www.youtube.com/c/coriwamsley

Jo Davis

Kindness is Badass

Jo Davis is an author, speaker, gifted intuitive guide, adventure addict, and the founder of Lift A Sister Up—an organization driven by the belief that our highest calling is to support and inspire other women to chase their dreams both personally and professionally. She is also a Reiki Master Teacher and a certified Death Doula.

Jo has over 150,000 followers and students. Believing that everyone has these powerful gifts, she shows ordinary people how to tap into their intuitive superpower through her course "Big Mess to Big Magic."

She is also a world-renowned artist and owner of Sky Soul Photography and Sky Soul Art, showcasing over a thousand pieces of work with clients worldwide.

Connect with Jo:

www.liftasisterup.com.

www.instagram.com/liftasisterup/

www.twitter.com/LiftASisterUp?s=0

www.facebook.com/skyjo73

www.clubhouse.com/@jodavis

Francesca Donlan

The $10 Kindness Club: Making Change with a Few Dollars

Francesca is deeply rooted in compassion and kindness. She is currently an adjunct professor at Florida Gulf Coast University teaching a course in kindness, which is one of the earliest of its kind and a model for courses in kindness across the nation. Additionally she continues to spread kindness through her Facebook group—

The $10 Kindness Club—which inspires members with ideas on how to give back with free or very low cost acts of kindness.

When she is not teaching, she serves as the communications director for the Lee County Visitor & Convention Bureau in Fort Myers, illustrating all of the best things to do in South West Florida and creating experiences for so many residents and visitors.

Prior to her position in public relations, she spent 20 years as a journalist working at newspapers throughout the country. She holds a bachelor's degree in psychology from Rutgers University and a master's degree in journalism from the University of Missouri.

Francesca demonstrates that there are always opportunities to spread positivity and is making the world a better place through her leadership in kindness and experiences.

Connect with Francesca:

www.facebook.com/francesca.donlan

www.facebook.com/groups/558353091718002 Or search @10-dollar-kindness-challenge

www.instagram.com/kindness.effect/

www.linkedin.com/in/francesca-donlan-08670563/

Magnus Wood

Billy Refused the Call

Hello. I'm Magnus Wood, founder of The Kindness Consultancy, author of *The Kindness Code*, and now proud co-author of *Living Kindly*!

I'm an ex adman, ex management consultant, ex managing director who now has the joy of helping create kinder places to work. Tired of working in too many toxic workplaces, I left my corporate career in 2019 to help organizations create cultures in which people thrive, do their best work, and create remarkable outcomes.

In the first COVID-19 lockdown, I explored the research, thinking, science, and wisdom around kindness. This led me to write a book, *The Kindness Code*. And now I work with businesses to unlock the power of kindness at work. I also co-host the podcast 'Little Shots of Kindness' with Cole; it's a mighty mix of unscripted conversation, data, science and optimism designed to inspire thought and instigate action to improve the connections we share and the outcomes we create, together.

I live on a narrow boat on the rivers of Southern England as well as a house in the New Forest, home to over 1,000 ancient trees, magical sites and incredible biodiversity. I'm also a TEDx host, yogi, cook, gin-maker and father of two beautiful daughters.

Connect with Magnus:

www.instagram.com/magnuswood/

www.twitter.com/magnuswood

www.magnuswood.com

Cole Baker Bagwell

Imagine (Do No Harm)

Cole Baker Bagwell (CB2) is the founder and chief kindness officer at Cool Audrey, a chief experience architect, writer, the host of the podcast Kindness Think Tank and the co-host of the podcast Little Shots of Kindness.

Cole spent two decades in the corporate world where she learned that every great business story begins with people, kindness makes people and business better, and the way we show up determines the relationships we cultivate and the outcomes we create—together.

Through her work, writing, and podcasts, Cole is raising awareness around the power of actionable kindness in transforming our collective experience and teaching people how to develop kindness as a core competency for business and life.

Connect with Cole:

cole@coolaudrey.com

www.coolaudrey.com/

LinkedIn www.linkedin.com/in/colebakerbagwell/

Kindness Think Tank Podcast www.coolaudrey.com/podcast

Little Shots of Kindness Podcast www.coolaudrey.com/little-shots-of-kindnes

Debbie Lundberg

Share Your Spare

Debbie Lundberg believes how you present is how you are remembered!

She is the founder and CEO of the Florida-based national firm Presenting Powerfully.

Debbie combined her 14-years of General Motors leadership with her 11-years of adjunct Dale Carnegie Training facilitation success during that same time frame to embark on her business endeavor to enhance communication, behaviors and relationships through four offerings: keynotes and talks, strategy and facilitation, teaming and training, and executive presence and public speaking coaching.

As an 11-time published author, certified virtual presenter, certified life coach, certified leadership coach, and certified image consultant, Debbie is a performance coach who writes a monthly business etiquette column for *Tampa Bay Business and Wealth Magazine*. Debbie also co-hosts The Business Of Life (TBOL) Master Class Podcast. Debbie's latest book, *REMOTE WORK ROCKSTAR*, quickly became the guidebook for working and leading virtually! A quick dose of Debbie can be seen in her 2020 TED Talk "Who CAREs."

Serving as a MacDill Air Force Base 927th Air Refueling Wing honorary commander board of directors member, South Tampa Chamber of Commerce board of directors member, Centre Club board of governors member (and former chair), Leadership Tampa alumnus, and The Special Needs Family Hour board member, Debbie is an active (three-year chair) member of the American Heart Association's Circle of Red, was honored as a 2020 South Tampa Chamber of Commerce Chamber Champion, and the 2021 South Tampa Chamber of Commerce Citizen of the Year.

Debbie was asked to join the Tampa General Hospital Patient and Advisory Council in 2020 after her kidney donation to a woman in need in Tampa Bay. Along with that, she has been a featured athlete in the Kidney Donor Athlete community. She mentors others who want to be living donors, including her husband, Michael, who donated six months after she did. Debbie's talks, classes, and workshops on kindness made her a good fit as a kindness attendant for Kindleigh's worldwide Kindness Community.

Debbie earned a B.A. in communication at the University of Michigan in Ann Arbor, Mich., and an M.B.A. at Edgewood College in Madison, Wisc.

Team Lundberg, which includes Michael and their four-legged daughters, two rescue labs, Lexi and Daisy, reside in South Tampa, where they settled in 2004.

Connect with Debbie:

Debbie@DebbieLundberg.com

www.debbielundberg.com/

www.linkedin.com/in/debbielundberg

www.podcasts.apple.com/us/podcast/the-business-of-life-master-class/id1458275356

https://twitter.com/DebbieLundberg

www.instagram.com/debbielundberg/

www.instagram.com/thebusinessoflifemasterclass/

www.debbielundberg.blogspot.com/

www.facebook.com/PresentingPowerfullyByDebbieLundberg

www.ted.com/talks/debbie_lundberg_who_cares

www.youtube.com/channel/UCK7A3W-yjctGmfpmclbDc3g

Daniel Levin

The Kindness of Listening

Levin walked away from an opportunity to run a billion dollar business, to hitchhike around the world to find happiness and inner peace. He studied in a seminary five years and left one day before becoming a rabbi, and he lived as a monk in a monastery for 10 years. As director of business development, he grew Hay House from $3,000,000 a year in sales to $100,000,000 a year in revenue.

Levin is rare blend of businessman and mystic who sees what others do not see. It has been this one quality more than any other that has thrown him into some of the most exclusive boardrooms to help companies innovate new ways of finding solutions when the old ways stop working.

He is the author of *The Mosaic*, a life changing fable that invites people to listen to those others do not hear and to see the situations in their life differently.

Connect with Daniel:

www.DanielBruceLevin.com

Krystle Mabery

A Kind Journey

Krystle Mabery is on a mission to create a space for people to thrive. A travel and food-loving neo-philanthropist, Krystle lives by the mentality of "If not me, then who?" Feeling innately compelled to step-up in the adversity of others, she places great intent on her role in the lives of others. In Corporate America, she discovered the value in understanding what motivates people. It was from this understanding that she was able to appeal to others, leading her to create and grow many successful partnerships and manage complex projects.

Although placing great value on her 10+ years of experience in hospitality and project management, Krystle was drawn toward a greater people-centered mission. At the peak of her career, Krystle made the bold, shocking decision to "not wait for someday" and begin a new chapter. Krystle's newfound purpose places inspiring and motivating others at the center of everything she does. Along this journey, she began creating opportunities to support others and embarked on new business endeavors mainly focusing on kindness in business training and coaching.

As a management consultant, Krystle brings a unique perspective to managing and growing a business that helps female entrepreneurs thrive in both their professional and personal lives. Krystle is an active (communications chair) member of the American Business Women's Association and was presented with a Certificate of Appreciation and challenge coin from the White House. A simple substitute teaching assignment, for Krystle, turned into an empowerment crusade to show the students that they each had potential. Living away from family in Florida, she spends her holidays donating food and time to those in need. Next steps for Krystle include partnering with a nonprofit dedicated to helping and assisting those who work in demanding workplaces mentally, physically, and emotionally.

Connect with Krystle:

www.linkedin.com/in/krystlemabery/

www.calendly.com/krystlemabery

www.facebook.com/krystlejmabery

www.instagram.com/live2_b_inspired/

Mark Shapiro

If not Kindness, What are We Influencing?

Former Showtime Networks exec Mark Shapiro is a heralded thought leader and international keynote speaker on the topics of human connection and kind leadership.

Mark is the CEO of Digital Humanity Inc, and the visionary behind the LoveBomb app—a first of its kind social wellness tool (for iOS) that helps you stay connected with your friends, family, and colleagues by creating a daily connection practice rooted in kindness and gratitude.

From sending over 12,000 appreciation videos, inspiring over 100,000 people to ignite meaningful 1-to-1 interactions, and giving the premiere TEDx talk on human connection in the digital age, Mark is at the forefront of social innovation.

Mark, and his groundbreaking work, has been seen on TEDx, CBS, and The School of Greatness Podcast; featured in publications such as *Entrepreneur*, Thrive Global, and *ENTITY Magazine*; and cited in multiple books including *Bring Your Whole Self To Work*, *Living Kindly*, and *Dear Gratitude*.

"In a world where we're used to leaders who don't follow through with their promises and companies that don't practice what they preach, Mark Shapiro and his work are a breath of fresh air." ~ *ENTITY Magazine*

To download the LoveBomb app, or share it with your team/communities, visit www.LoveBomb.app.

For speaking, relationship building workshops, and consulting, book a discovery call with Mark at www.calendly.com/kindbiz.

Connect with Mark:

www.instagram.com/areyoubeingreal/

www.instagram.com/lovebomb.app/

Angelica Perman

Kindhearted: How I Healed a Broken Heart

Angelica is a global intuitive guide; spiritual coach for addiction, trauma recovery, and self-care; #1 bestselling author; and sound healer.

She offers one-on-one private spiritual coaching, clearing, sound baths, ceremonies, and online classes for spiritual support, recovery, and intuitive development. Angelica is an award-winning musician and will be releasing multiple original musical projects and launching a tour. She exudes kindness and helps people step into their light.

Connect with Angelica:

www.angelicaperman.com

www.instagram.com/AngelicaPerman

www.instagram.com/thesoundempress/

Jonathan Darling

Micro-Moments: Massive Impact

Jonathan Darling is focused on making an impact in the world through Micro-Moments. He challenges the notion that acts of kindness should be random—rather he sees the opportunity to teach others how to make kindness an all day, every day practice. I encourage you to add him to your network.

Here is a little more about him:

"You're never going to make anything out of your life."

"You know nothing about leadership."

"You just need to stay in your lane and stop writing about things you know nothing about."

"Why would anyone want to hear you speak about leadership when you're not a leader?"

These are just some of the comments I've had said to me throughout my life. But it is these comments that help drive me and my passion to help others understand the true purpose of leadership.

From leading teams, to speaking for organizations and universities, I strive to empower individuals to lead, not from position or title, but from their heart. I teach that leadership is truly loving and caring for the people around them, influencing positive change and being the catalyst for self-belief in their lives. I help people focus on the Micro-Moments that can have a massive impact.

Connect with Jonathan:

www.instagram.com/thejonathandarling/

www.facebook.com/The-Jonathan-Darling-103721065127055

www.linkedin.com/in/jonathandarling44

www.jonathandarling.net_

Made in the USA
Monee, IL
30 July 2021